AF266850

Systematic Theology for Beginners 5-in-1

A Simple Guide to God, Humanity, Salvation, the Spirit, and the Future

TABLE OF CONTENTS

OVERALL INTRODUCTION

Start Systematic Theology with Confidence: What It Is, Why It Matters, and How to Use This 5-in-1 Guide

Systematic theology sounds like a classroom word. Many believers hear it and picture thick books, long footnotes, and debates they did not ask for. Yet the basic idea is simple. Systematic theology is the careful practice of gathering what the whole Bible teaches about a topic, then stating it clearly and faithfully. It helps you connect Scripture's many parts into one coherent confession.

Every Christian already does some form of theology. When you say "God is good," you are making a theological claim. When you say "Jesus saves," you are making another. The question is not whether you will form beliefs. The question is whether your beliefs will be shaped by Scripture or by habit, emotion, culture, or personal preference. Scripture calls believers to grow in knowledge that leads to love and steady obedience (Colossians 1:9–10). That growth does not happen by accident.

This book exists for readers who want clarity without pretension. You may be new to the Bible. You may have been in church for years but still feel unsure when hard questions come. You may love God deeply and still struggle to explain what you believe. This guide aims to help you speak with conviction and humility, because your foundation is the Word of God.

What Systematic Theology Is (and What It Is Not)

Systematic theology is not a replacement for reading the Bible. It is not a shortcut around prayer, worship, and discipleship. It is a tool that supports them. It gathers the Bible's teaching the way a good map gathers roads. The roads are still real places. The map simply helps you see how they connect.

Systematic theology is also not an excuse to win arguments. The goal is not to sound clever. The goal is to know God, love Him, and live faithfully. Scripture warns against knowledge that inflates pride (1 Corinthians 8:1). At the same time, Scripture commands believers to handle the Word with care and to guard the truth once delivered to the saints (2 Timothy 2:15; Jude 1:3). A healthy theology produces steadiness, worship, repentance, and courage.

A simple way to define systematic theology is this: it is Bible truth organized for faithful living. It takes doctrine out of the clouds and puts it into daily decisions.

Why This Matters for Real Life

Bad theology does not stay on a page. It shows up in the way we pray, the way we raise children, the way we treat money, and the way we face suffering. If we view God as distant, our prayers shrink. If we view people as accidents, human dignity weakens. If we treat salvation as self-improvement, guilt never lifts. If we treat the Holy Spirit as a vague force, we become confused about guidance and holiness. If we treat the future as unclear or irrelevant, hope fades and fear rises.

Good theology also does not stay on a page. It shapes the heart. It strengthens faith under pressure. It steadies believers who feel tossed around by social media claims, sensational teachers, and shifting moral norms. Scripture itself ties doctrine to stability: believers should no longer be like children, carried by every wind of teaching (Ephesians 4:14). That is not a call to suspicion. It is a call to maturity.

Here is the promise of this book: if you learn to think biblically about God, humanity, salvation, the Spirit, and the future, you will gain a stronger grip on reality. You will also gain a gentler posture toward others, because you will know the difference between essential truths and secondary debates.

One Question You Might Be Asking

Do I need theology if I just want to love Jesus? Yes, because the Jesus you love must be the Jesus Scripture reveals. Love is not sustained by sentiment alone. Love grows when truth becomes clear, and when trust becomes deeper. The Bible does not separate love from knowledge. It joins them.

How This 5-in-1 Guide Is Built

This volume is arranged as five "Books" inside one collection. Each chapter is written for beginners, but it does not treat you like a child. The chapters aim for plain speech, clear structure, and direct application.

Scripture First, Then Clear Reasoning

This book is Biblically centered by design. We treat Scripture as the final authority for doctrine. That does not mean we ignore church history. It means we place church history in its proper role. Christians have wrestled with doctrine for two thousand years. Councils, creeds, and confessions often clarify what Scripture teaches, especially when false views arise. For example, the early church fought for clear language about the Trinity and the full deity and humanity of Christ. Those were not academic games. They were matters of worship and salvation.

So, throughout this book, you will see careful use of church history. You will see how faithful believers argued, where they agreed, and why certain conclusions became standard. You will also see where Christians differ today on secondary matters. In those places, you will be given the strongest biblical arguments on each side, with a steady emphasis on charity and truth.

We will also define key terms in plain language. Systematic theology uses words like "attribute," "incarnation," "atonement," "justification," and "sanctification." These words can feel heavy at first. But they exist because they serve clarity. When you learn them, you can speak precisely, and you can avoid confusion that harms faith.

The Method You Will Learn (So You Can Keep Growing)

You will repeatedly practice a simple method:

1. **Gather the relevant Scriptures.**

   We look at passages that directly teach the topic.

2. **Read each passage in context.**

   One verse should not be forced to say what it does not say.

3. **Summarize the Bible's teaching in one clear statement.**

   We aim for faithful sentences, not slogans.

4. **Test that statement against the whole Bible.**

   Scripture does not contradict itself.

5. **Apply the doctrine to worship, obedience, and endurance.**

   Truth is meant to shape life.

If you learn this method, you will not depend on a single teacher. You will become a steady reader of Scripture who can evaluate claims with care.

A Word About Disagreements

Some doctrines are non-negotiable in historic Christianity. The Trinity is essential. The true humanity and true deity of Christ are essential. Salvation by grace, through faith, because of Christ's work, is essential. The bodily resurrection of Jesus is essential. God's final judgment and the promised renewal of creation are essential.

Other doctrines have faithful Christian disagreement. Timing details about end-times events often fall here. Some questions about spiritual gifts, church governance, and baptism practices also vary across traditions. This book will treat essential truths with firmness. It will treat secondary matters with honesty and respect. You do not need to fear those differences. You need to learn how to sort them.

What is the point of learning both agreement and disagreement? It helps you avoid two common errors. The first error is to treat every issue as equally important, which leads to constant conflict. The second error is to treat no issue as important, which leads to drifting and confusion. Scripture calls for both conviction and love.

How to Use This Book Well

If you read alone, take one chapter at a time. Do not rush. After each chapter, answer the discussion questions in writing. If possible, speak your answers out loud. Doctrine settles into the mind when we put words to it.

If you read with a group or family, set a weekly rhythm. Read a chapter during the week. Then meet for 45–60 minutes. Start with prayer. End with one specific action step. For example, after a chapter on God's holiness, you might choose a focused confession of sin and a plan to reconcile a strained relationship. After a chapter on providence, you might choose to pray through a current worry in a more structured way.

If you are a teacher or ministry leader, use the chapters as a framework. Each chapter is structured to support teaching. You can expand the Scripture reading, add historical quotes, and bring in examples from pastoral life.

What You Can Expect as You Read

You should expect your mind to sharpen. You should also expect your heart to be confronted. Biblical truth does both. Scripture often comforts, but it also corrects. It warns, it invites, and it calls for change. If you encounter a doctrine that challenges your assumptions, do not panic. Slow down. Return to Scripture. Pray for humility and clarity. God honors honest seeking.

You should also expect to gain confidence without arrogance. Confidence comes from knowing that your beliefs are rooted in God's Word, not in personal mood. Arrogance comes from forgetting that everything we know is received. The posture of a student never ends. Even the most mature believer remains a learner.

This book uses the **NSV** for Scripture references unless otherwise noted. When we cite a passage, the goal is not to sprinkle verses on top of our ideas. The goal is to let Scripture lead. Theology is faithful only when it echoes God's voice.

One more question: what if you feel unqualified to study theology? You are qualified if you belong to Christ and you are willing to learn. Scripture was given to the church, not only to scholars. The Spirit teaches believers through the Word, within the life of the church (John 16:13; Acts 2:42). Begin with humility, consistency, and a desire to obey.

Now we start where Scripture starts: with God. The most practical thing you can do for your life is to know Him as He truly is.

BOOK ONE
KNOW THE LIVING GOD

A Simple Guide to God's Being, Words, Works, and Ways

CHAPTER 1

BEGIN WITH GOD'S SELF - REVELATION: LEARN HOW GOD MAKES HIMSELF KNOWN

If you want to know God, you must start with a simple fact: God is not silent. We do not climb our way up to Him by intelligence, effort, or emotion. God makes Himself known because He chooses to do so. The Bible does not present faith as guessing. It presents faith as hearing God's voice and responding.

Hebrews 1:1-2 (NSV) sets the tone. God spoke in many ways in earlier times, and He has spoken with final clarity in His Son. That means Christianity stands or falls on revelation. If God does not reveal Himself, then theology becomes speculation. If God does reveal Himself, then theology becomes obedience: we learn, we worship, and we live in line with what He has shown.

1) Define Revelation the Way Scripture Does

Revelation means "making known what would otherwise remain hidden." The key idea is not that humans discover God. The key idea is that God discloses Himself. He shows His character, His will, and His saving plan.

Deuteronomy 29:29 (NSV) makes a crucial distinction. Some things belong to God alone, but what He has revealed belongs to His people so they can obey. This verse protects you from two opposite mistakes. One mistake is to demand answers God has not given. The other mistake is to neglect what God has clearly said.

So revelation is both a gift and a boundary. It is a gift because God gives real knowledge of Himself. It is a boundary because God sets the limits of what we can know.

Do you need to know everything about God to know Him truly? No, because God gives true knowledge without giving exhaustive knowledge. A child can know a parent truly without knowing every detail of the parent's life.

That is how Scripture trains our minds. God is infinite. We are creatures. We can know Him truly because He speaks truly. We cannot know Him fully because we are not God.

2) Learn the Two Main Categories: General and Special Revelation

Christians often use two terms that help organize the Bible's teaching: **general revelation** and **special revelation**.

General Revelation: God Makes His Existence and Power Plain

General revelation refers to what God shows through creation and providence. Psalm 19:1–4 (NSV) teaches that the created order communicates God's glory. Romans 1:19–20 (NSV) teaches that God's invisible attributes are seen through what He has made, so people are accountable.

General revelation is real, constant, and universal. Everyone lives in God's world. Everyone receives breath, food, seasons, and the order of nature. God's power and wisdom shine through what He made.

But general revelation has limits. It can tell you that God exists, that He is powerful, that He rules, and that you are responsible to Him. It cannot tell you the gospel. It does not tell you the name of the Savior, the meaning of the cross, or the promise of forgiveness. It can expose guilt, but it cannot cleanse guilt.

That is why Scripture never treats nature as a substitute for God's Word. Creation points. Scripture explains.

Special Revelation: God Speaks for Salvation and Covenant Life

Special revelation refers to God's direct self-disclosure through His spoken and written Word, fulfilled in Jesus Christ. Hebrews 1:1–2 (NSV) highlights both the diversity of God's past communication and the finality of His revelation in the Son.

Special revelation includes God's words through prophets and apostles. It includes God's mighty acts interpreted by God's own speech. It includes Scripture as the written, enduring form of that revelation. And it reaches its center in the person and work of Jesus.

John 1:18 (NSV) teaches that the Son makes the Father known. This is decisive. God does not merely send information. He sends His Son. Christianity is not first a set of ideas. It is God giving Himself to us through Christ, then giving words that explain that gift.

3) See Why Sin Makes Revelation Necessary and Grace Makes It Possible

If humans were morally neutral, they might respond to God's world with clear-eyed gratitude. But Scripture teaches that sin twists perception. Romans 1 does not describe people as lacking evidence. It describes people as suppressing the truth. Sin does not merely break rules. Sin bends the heart away from God.

That means revelation is not only about information. It is about rescue. God does not speak because He is lonely. He speaks because He is gracious and because we need truth to live.

You also need to understand another point: even special revelation does not produce faith automatically. People can hear God's words and still resist. That is why Scripture also speaks about the Spirit's work of illumination. 1 Corinthians 2:10–12 (NSV) teaches that God's Spirit helps believers grasp what God has given.

4) Learn the Main Ways God Reveals Himself in Scripture

God reveals Himself through several channels across redemptive history. The Bible does not flatten them into one method. It shows God speaking and acting in complementary ways.

God Reveals Himself Through His Names

Names in Scripture often carry meaning. In Exodus 3:14 (NSV), God identifies Himself in a way that emphasizes His self-existence and faithfulness. He is not defined by the world. He is not dependent on anything outside Himself. He simply is.

This matters for beginners because it clears away common errors. God is not a larger version of you. God is not a force inside nature. God is personal, living, and free. He stands over creation as Creator, and He draws near by covenant grace.

God Reveals Himself Through His Acts

God's works interpret God's character. Creation displays His wisdom and generosity. The exodus displays His power to save and His commitment to His promises. Judgment displays His justice. Provision displays His care.

But here is the key: Scripture does not leave God's acts open to personal interpretation. God often explains His acts with His words. He tells Israel what the exodus means. He tells the church what the cross means. He tells believers what the resurrection means.

If you separate acts from words, you will misread the acts. If you receive acts through God's words, you will learn to worship rather than speculate.

God Reveals Himself Through His Spoken Word

Throughout the Bible, God speaks. He speaks commands, promises, warnings, and comfort. He speaks in covenant language: "I will be your God, and you will be my people." His speech is not casual. His speech creates obligations and hope.

God's spoken Word also exposes the heart. When God speaks, you learn what you love, what you fear, and what you excuse. That is why Scripture often feels personal. It is personal, because God addresses persons.

God Reveals Himself Through Scripture as Written Word

God's revelation did not end as scattered memories. God gave Scripture as an enduring witness. 2 Peter 1:20–21 (NSV) teaches that prophecy did not arise from human initiative, but from God's Spirit moving human authors.

This is where systematic theology begins to feel practical. If Scripture is God's written Word, then you have a stable source of truth. You do not need to chase rumors, impulses, or trending voices. You can open your Bible and read what God has spoken.

5) Hold to Four Commitments That Keep You Steady

If you want to grow without drifting, commit to four simple principles. These principles show up across historic Christian teaching because they reflect how Scripture functions.

Commitment 1: Treat Scripture as Your Highest Authority

Many voices compete for authority: personal experience, family tradition, cultural pressure, and even fear. Scripture must govern them all. This does not mean you despise learning. It means you test every claim by God's Word.

When a belief conflicts with Scripture, Scripture wins. When a practice contradicts Scripture, Scripture corrects it.

Commitment 2: Read Passages in Context

A single verse can be misunderstood when you detach it from its chapter, its book, and the full storyline of Scripture. Context protects you from forcing Scripture to support ideas it does not teach.

This also guards you from shallow reading. God's Word is coherent. Themes repeat. Promises develop. Fulfillment arrives in Christ. You will understand more when you read whole sections, not only isolated lines.

Commitment 3: Let Clear Passages Interpret Less Clear Passages

Scripture contains poetry, visions, and difficult statements. Do not build a major doctrine on an unclear verse. Use the plain teaching of Scripture to guide your reading of the harder parts.

This principle reduces confusion and conflict. It also increases confidence, because the Bible speaks plainly about the truths that matter most.

Commitment 4: Connect Revelation to Worship and Obedience

The goal is not to store facts. The goal is to know God and honor Him. True knowledge produces reverence. It also produces repentance, gratitude, patience, and courage.

If your study makes you harsh, you are studying wrongly. If your study makes you prayerless, you are studying wrongly. Scripture aims for faith working through love.

6) Avoid Common Traps That Disfigure Theology

Beginners often face predictable dangers. Naming them helps you resist them.

Trap 1: Treat Feelings as Revelation

Feelings matter, but they do not define truth. A strong impression may be wisdom, fear, habit, or temptation. God may comfort you through Scripture, but that comfort comes through His Word, not apart from it.

So measure impressions by Scripture. If the impression contradicts Scripture, reject it. If it aligns with Scripture, hold it with humility, and seek wise counsel.

Trap 2: Treat Theology as a Private Project

God reveals Himself to form a people. Scripture assumes community: worship, teaching, correction, and shared life. If you try to build doctrine alone, you will likely build blind spots into your beliefs.

Read Scripture personally, yes. But also learn within the church. Listen to faithful teachers. Study the great creeds and confessions as summaries, not as replacements. Let the body of Christ sharpen you.

Trap 3: Demand Certainty Where Scripture Allows Humble Patience

Some questions have firm answers. Others require careful thought and charity. Wisdom knows the difference.

When Scripture is clear, speak clearly. When Scripture is less specific, speak carefully. Do not turn opinions into tests of fellowship. At the same time, do not use "mystery" as an excuse for laziness.

CHAPTER 2

CONFESS ONE GOD IN THREE PERSONS: GRASP THE TRINITY WITHOUT CONFUSION

Christians are often told the Trinity is "too advanced" for ordinary believers. Scripture disagrees. The Bible does not hide God's identity behind a locked door. It calls God's people to worship Him as He truly is. If you want to pray with confidence, read the Bible with clarity, and guard the gospel from distortion, you must understand the Trinity.

The Trinity does not mean "three gods." It does not mean "one person wearing three masks." It means the one true God eternally exists as three distinct persons: Father, Son, and Holy Spirit. God is one in being, and three in person. That is the Christian confession.

This chapter will help you say that confession with understanding. We will build from Scripture first. Then we will use careful language shaped by the church's early teaching. We will also name common errors and show why they fail.

1) Start Where the Bible Starts: God Is One

The Bible is clear that there is only one God. Deuteronomy 6:4 (NSV) states it plainly: the Lord is one. This is not a minor theme. It is the foundation of biblical faith. Israel was called to worship the one Creator, not the many gods of the nations. The church inherits that same confession.

So any explanation of the Trinity must protect monotheism. The Trinity does not add gods. It clarifies the identity of the one God who saves.

A helpful way to state this first truth is simple: **Christianity is strict monotheism.** There is one God, not three.

While Scripture insists God is one, it also speaks of the Father, Son, and Spirit in ways that cannot be reduced to mere titles or roles.

One of the clearest places is the command of Jesus in Matthew 28:19 (NSV). He tells His disciples to baptize in the name of the Father, and of the Son, and of the Holy Spirit. Notice "name" is singular. Yet three are named. Jesus does not treat Father, Son, and Spirit as three separate deities. He places them together under the one divine name.

Another key text is 2 Corinthians 13:14 (NSV). Paul blesses the church with grace from the Lord Jesus Christ, love from God, and fellowship of the Holy Spirit. This is not casual language. The church's life is described as coming from the Father, through the Son, in the Spirit.

This pattern appears across the New Testament. Christians did not invent it later. They recognized what Scripture already gave them.

3) Affirm What Scripture Affirms About the Son

The Trinity becomes clearer when you see what Scripture teaches about Jesus. The Son is not a created helper. The Son is not a lesser deity. The Son is fully God, and truly distinct from the Father.

John 1:1–3 (NSV) teaches that the Word was with God and was God, and that all things were made through Him. This guards two truths at once. First, the Son is truly God. Second, the Son is personally distinct, because He is "with" God.

Jesus also receives honors that belong to God alone. In John 20:28 (NSV), Thomas addresses Jesus as "my Lord and my God." Jesus does not correct him. He receives that confession.

Hebrews speaks of the Son as the exact imprint of God's nature and the one who upholds all things (Hebrews 1:3, NSV). That is divine work. Creatures do not uphold the universe.

So Scripture forces a decision. If you take the Bible seriously, you cannot treat Jesus as merely a moral teacher or a high angel. He is the eternal Son.

4) Affirm What Scripture Affirms About the Holy Spirit

Many believers understand the Father and the Son but remain unsure about the Spirit. Scripture will not allow the Spirit to be treated as an "it" or as a mere force.

In Acts 5:3–4 (NSV), Peter confronts Ananias. He says Ananias has lied to the Holy Spirit, and then he says Ananias has lied to God. The Spirit can be lied to because He is personal. The Spirit is identified with God because He is divine.

The Spirit also acts with divine authority. He speaks, directs, appoints, and searches the depths of God (see Acts 13:2; 1 Corinthians 2:10–11, NSV). These are not descriptions of impersonal energy. They are descriptions of a divine person.

5) Use Careful Words: One Being, Three Persons

Once you see Scripture's teaching, the next step is to speak about it accurately. The church did not create the Trinity out of thin air. It created language to protect what Scripture teaches and to reject false summaries.

Here is the classic wording that helps most beginners:

- **There is one God in being (or essence).**
- **There are three persons: Father, Son, and Holy Spirit.**
- **The persons are distinct, not identical.**
- **The persons are not three gods, because the being is one.**

"Being" answers the question, "What is God?" The answer: God is one.

"Person" answers the question, "Who is God?" The answer: Father, Son, and Spirit.

This is careful, but it is not complicated once you practice it. It is also necessary. If you blur "being" and "person," you will fall into error quickly.

6) Learn from History: Why the Creeds Matter

In the early centuries, the church faced teachers who claimed to honor Scripture while denying its meaning. Two major errors forced the church to speak with precision.

Arianism taught that the Son was the first and greatest created being. This view sounded respectful, but it destroyed salvation. A created savior cannot bring you to God. Only God can save. The church answered with the Council of Nicaea (AD 325), confessing that the Son is of the same essence as the Father.

Later, the church clarified the Spirit's full divinity more explicitly at Constantinople (AD 381). The result is what many call the Nicene Creed, a summary meant to guard biblical teaching in worship and instruction.

Why does this matter for you today? Because the same old errors return with new packaging. Creeds help you recognize them quickly. They also show you that the Trinity is not a modern theory. It is the church's settled reading of Scripture.

7) Reject Three Common Errors

If you can name the common mistakes, you can avoid them.

Error 1: Modalism (One Person, Three Masks)

Modalism says God is one person who appears sometimes as Father, sometimes as Son, sometimes as Spirit. This fails because Scripture shows the persons relating to one another at the same time. At Jesus' baptism, the Son is baptized, the Spirit descends, and the Father speaks from heaven (Matthew 3:16–17, NSV). That is not one person acting three parts in sequence. It is three persons acting together.

Error 2: Tritheism (Three Separate Gods)

Tritheism treats Father, Son, and Spirit as three independent divine beings. This fails because Scripture insists God is one. The Father, Son, and Spirit share one divine life, one will, and one glory. Christianity is not a committee of deities. It is the worship of the one true God.

Error 3: Subordinationism (Son and Spirit as Lesser Deities)

Some say the Son and Spirit are divine, but not fully divine. Scripture does not speak that way. The Son creates and rules all things. The Spirit is identified with God and acts with God's authority. To reduce their divinity is to rewrite the Bible.

8) Handle Illustrations with Caution

Many people try to explain the Trinity with simple pictures. Most of them mislead.

Water as ice, liquid, and steam suggests one substance shifting forms. That leans toward modalism. The three-leaf clover suggests three parts that make a whole. That leans toward tritheism or partialism, as if each person is one-third of God.

Is there any illustration that works perfectly? No, because God is not like anything in creation. Creation can hint. It cannot match.

So use illustrations only as temporary supports, and always return to Scripture's words. The Trinity is not a puzzle to solve. It is a truth to confess.

9) Understand the Trinity in Salvation

The Trinity is not an abstract doctrine. It is the shape of the gospel.

- The **Father** plans salvation and sends the Son (John 3:16, NSV).
- The **Son** accomplishes salvation through His life, death, and resurrection (Romans 5:8–10, NSV).
- The **Spirit** applies salvation by giving new birth and uniting us to Christ (Titus 3:5–6, NSV).

This means your salvation is not a vague kindness from an unknown deity. It is the coordinated work of the triune God. The Father's love is not separate from the Son's grace. The Spirit's work is not detached from the Father's purpose. One God saves, in a triune manner.

Here is a practical result: when you struggle with assurance, the Trinity steadies you. The Father chose to save. The Son finished the saving work. The Spirit brings that finished work home to your heart. Your hope rests on God's action, not your mood.

10) Pray and Worship as a Trinitarian Christian

Many believers say they believe in the Trinity, but they do not practice trinitarian worship. Scripture teaches you to pray to the Father, through the Son, by the Spirit. This is not a rule meant to limit your words. It is a pattern meant to deepen your reverence and confidence.

When you pray to the Father, you approach the source of every good gift. When you pray through the Son, you rely on the one mediator who brings you near. When you pray by the Spirit, you depend on the one who helps you in weakness and shapes your desires toward holiness (Romans 8:26–27, NSV).

This also shapes church worship. Christian worship is directed to the Father, centered on the Son, and empowered by the Spirit. If you remove any person, you damage the whole.

11) Speak with Humility and Confidence

The Trinity is a mystery in one sense: you could never invent it. It is also clear in another sense: Scripture teaches it, and the church confesses it. Mystery does not mean confusion. It means God is greater than our categories.

So be humble. Do not pretend to explain God fully. But also be confident. God has revealed enough for worship, faith, and obedience.

A good summary you can remember is this:

The Father is God. The Son is God. The Spirit is God.

The Father is not the Son. The Son is not the Spirit. The Spirit is not the Father.

There is one God.

CHAPTER 3

TRUST GOD'S CHARACTER: STUDY HIS HOLINESS, LOVE, JUSTICE, AND MERCY

Many people believe in "a god" who feels like them, changes like them, and excuses what they excuse. Scripture will not let us settle for that. The living God reveals His character so we can trust Him, fear Him, and draw near to Him with clean hands and steady hope.

This chapter focuses on four core traits that Scripture highlights again and again: **holiness, love, justice, and mercy**. These traits do not compete. They belong together. If you pull them apart, you will misread God and misunderstand the gospel.

1) Begin with Holiness: God Is Set Apart and Morally Pure

Holiness means God is set apart from all creation and morally perfect in all He is and does. Holiness is not one attribute among many. Scripture often presents it as the "atmosphere" of God's presence.

Isaiah 6:1–3 (NSV) gives a famous scene. Isaiah sees the Lord high and exalted. Seraphim call out, "Holy, holy, holy." They repeat the word three times, not because they lack vocabulary, but because holiness stands at the center of God's revealed majesty. The vision does more than inform Isaiah. It crushes his pride and exposes his sin. He responds with confession because holiness reveals reality.

God's holiness means He never bends toward evil. He never adjusts His standards to fit our excuses. He never grows numb to sin. Scripture says, "Be holy, for I am holy" (1 Peter 1:15–16, NSV). That command does not imply we can become divine. It means God's moral purity sets the standard for His people.

Holiness also guards you from sentimental theology. Some people speak as if love means God ignores evil. Scripture rejects that. Holiness means God's love never becomes moral indifference.

2) Understand Love Correctly: God Gives Himself for Our Good

Scripture teaches that God is love (1 John 4:8, NSV). That statement is often quoted, and often misused. Many people define love as approval. Scripture defines love as holy self-giving that seeks the true good of the beloved.

In 1 John 4:9–10 (NSV), love appears in action. God shows love by sending His Son. The text ties love to atonement, not to vague kindness. God's love does not float above sin. It deals with sin through sacrifice.

This protects you from another error: treating love as God's only defining trait. God is love, but God is not only love in the way modern culture uses the word. Biblical love works with holiness and justice. It does not erase them.

Church history helps here. Pastors and theologians often said God's love is not random affection. It is covenant faithfulness. God commits Himself to His people and keeps His promise even at great cost. That is why Scripture links love to God's steadfast love and faithfulness, not merely to His emotions.

3) Hold to Justice: God Always Does What Is Right

God's justice means He always acts in perfect righteousness. He judges without corruption. He shows no partiality. He never makes mistakes. He never "grades on a curve." He does what is right because He is right.

Psalm 89:14 (NSV) says righteousness and justice are the foundation of God's throne. That means God's rule rests on moral perfection, not raw power. God does not rule like a tyrant. He rules like a righteous King.

God's justice also explains why Scripture takes sin seriously. If God shrugged at evil, He would not be good. If He ignored oppression, He would not be righteous. If He excused lies, violence, and abuse without judgment, He would become the opposite of the God the Bible reveals.

This matters in daily life. When you see injustice in your home, workplace, or nation, you may feel rage, despair, or cynicism. God's justice gives you another option: you can grieve honestly and still refuse despair. God sees. God knows. God will judge.

Romans 2:6–8 (NSV) teaches that God repays each person according to deeds. Scripture never uses this truth to produce smugness. It uses it to call for repentance and to assure the oppressed that evil will not have the last word.

4) Receive Mercy: God Shows Compassion to the Guilty and Weak

Mercy means God's compassion toward those who deserve judgment and cannot rescue themselves. Mercy does not deny guilt. Mercy addresses guilt with grace.

Exodus 34:6–7 (NSV) stands among the clearest places where God describes Himself. God declares that He is compassionate and gracious, slow to anger, and abounding in steadfast love. In the same breath, He also says He will not clear the guilty. That combination is not a contradiction. It is the tension Scripture forces us to hold until we see its fullest resolution in the saving work God provides.

Mercy also appears in daily faithfulness. Lamentations 3:22–23 (NSV) says God's steadfast love does not cease, and His mercies are new each morning. That statement comes from the middle of suffering and ruin. The writer does not deny pain. He affirms mercy within pain.

Many believers think mercy is only for the moment of conversion. Scripture treats mercy as God's ongoing posture toward His people. Mercy sustains the weak, restores the repentant, and invites the sinner to return.

5) Refuse to Separate What God Joins

Here is where many Christians get stuck. Some emphasize holiness and justice but forget love and mercy. Their theology becomes cold, suspicious, and harsh. Others emphasize love and mercy but downplay holiness and justice. Their theology becomes sentimental and permissive.

Scripture joins the traits. God's holiness does not cancel His love. God's love does not cancel His justice. God's justice does not cancel His mercy. God's mercy does not cancel His holiness.

Micah 6:8 (NSV) gives a simple pattern for God-centered living: do justice, love mercy, and walk humbly with your God. Notice the balance. Justice and mercy belong together. Humility keeps you from using either one as a weapon.

James 2:13 (NSV) adds another helpful note: mercy triumphs over judgment. The context does not erase judgment. It condemns favoritism and calls God's people to reflect God's heart. Mercy "triumphs" because God does not leave repentant sinners under condemnation. He provides a way to forgive and restore without abandoning righteousness.

6) See How the Cross Holds These Truths Together

The clearest display of God's character appears where many people least expect it: in the suffering and death of Jesus Christ. At the cross, God does not choose between justice and mercy. He reveals both.

Romans 3:25–26 (NSV) explains that God presented Christ as a sacrifice of atonement. The purpose is moral clarity. God shows His righteousness, and He justifies the one who has faith. This matters because forgiveness is not God pretending sin did not happen. Forgiveness is God dealing with sin in a way that satisfies righteousness and grants mercy.

This is why the gospel is not moral advice. It is divine action. God remains just, and God shows mercy. God keeps His holiness intact, and God extends love to sinners.

When you understand this, you gain a strong answer to two common fears:

- The fear that God is too holy to receive you.
- The fear that God is too kind to correct you.

The cross answers both. God receives repentant sinners because He provides cleansing. God corrects His people because He loves them enough to make them holy.

7) Learn to Trust God's Character in Real Situations

Doctrine becomes valuable when it steadies you under pressure.

When you feel condemned: remember God's mercy and love. Confess sin with honesty. Do not hide. God calls you into light so He can restore you.

When you feel casual about sin: remember God's holiness and justice. Do not treat grace as permission. Grace trains you to obey.

When you suffer unfair treatment: remember God's justice. You can pursue help, seek protection, and speak truth without sinking into bitterness. God's throne rests on righteousness.

When you doubt God's goodness: remember that Scripture defines goodness by God's character, not by your comfort. God's love remains steady even when circumstances feel confusing. Mercy does not mean an easy path. Mercy means God does not abandon His people.

A mature Christian learns to say, with calm confidence, that God is good even when life hurts. That confidence does not come from denial. It comes from knowing God's character.

8) Practice a Simple "Four-Part" Worship Pattern

If you want these truths to shape your life, apply them in worship. Use a four-part pattern in prayer:

1. **Praise God for His holiness** (reverence).
2. **Thank God for His love** (gratitude).
3. **Submit to God's justice** (humility and integrity).
4. **Ask God for mercy** (confession and help).

CHAPTER 4

RECEIVE GOD'S WORD: UNDERSTAND INSPIRATION, AUTHORITY, AND CLARITY OF SCRIPTURE

If you want to know God rightly, you must know how He speaks. Christians do not treat the Bible as a helpful religious guide among many. We treat it as God's written Word. That single conviction shapes everything else: how we worship, how we make choices, how we correct sin, and how we endure suffering.

Many people today respect the Bible in theory but ignore it in practice. Others read it but do not trust it. Some treat it like a book of inspiring thoughts. Some treat it like a codebook for winning arguments. Scripture calls us to a better posture: hear God's voice, submit to it, and live by it.

This chapter will explain three closely linked truths: **inspiration** (where Scripture comes from), **authority** (what Scripture requires), and **clarity** (how Scripture speaks). We will also look at how the church has defended these truths across history, and how you can read the Bible with confidence and care.

1) Start with Inspiration: Scripture Is God-Breathed

The central text for inspiration is 2 Timothy 3:16–17 (NSV). It teaches that all Scripture is God-breathed and useful for teaching, correction, and training in righteousness, so God's people are equipped for good works.

"God-breathed" means Scripture originates from God. It does not mean the human authors became robots. It means God spoke through human writers in such a way that what they wrote is truly God's Word.

2 Peter 1:20–21 (NSV) adds important detail. Prophecy did not come

by human will. Men spoke from God as they were moved by the Holy Spirit. The Spirit's work did not erase personality, style, or historical context. It ensured the final message was God's intended Word.

This protects you from two mistakes:

- **Mistake one:** treating the Bible as a merely human book that can be dismissed when it conflicts with preference.
- **Mistake two:** treating the Bible as if God dropped it from heaven without human language, history, or genre.

Inspiration means God used real people, in real times, using real words, to communicate a message that is fully trustworthy.

2) Understand What Inspiration Does and Does Not Mean

Inspiration does not mean every biblical writer knew every implication of what they wrote. It also does not mean every verse is equally easy to interpret. The Bible contains poetry, narrative, prophecy, proverbs, letters, and visions. Each genre communicates in its own way.

Inspiration does mean that Scripture is reliable in what it teaches. Jesus treats Scripture this way. He quotes it as decisive. He appeals to it as the final court. He teaches that Scripture cannot be broken (John 10:35, NSV).

The apostles do the same. They reason from Scripture, correct error by Scripture, and call the church to submit to Scripture. The pattern is consistent: God speaks, and God's people listen.

3) Move to Authority: Scripture Carries God's Right to Command

Authority means Scripture is not merely informative. It is binding. When Scripture speaks, God speaks. That is why Scripture carries the right to correct you even when you disagree.

A key passage is 1 Thessalonians 2:13 (NSV). Paul thanks God that the believers received the apostolic message not as the word of men, but as what it truly is: the word of God, which works in those who believe. The church is not free to treat Scripture as optional. Scripture addresses the church with God's authority.

Authority also means you cannot place your conscience above the

Word. Your conscience matters, but it is not infallible. It can be misinformed or hardened. Scripture is the standard that informs the conscience. When conscience and Scripture conflict, Scripture corrects conscience.

This is one reason Christians have historically emphasized preaching. Preaching is not entertainment. It is the public reading and explanation of God's Word so God's people can obey.

4) Receive Scripture as Sufficient for Faith and Life

Another key principle is sufficiency. Sufficiency means Scripture contains everything necessary for salvation and godly living. It does not contain every fact about science, medicine, or engineering. It does contain everything you need to know God, trust Christ, repent of sin, and walk in obedience.

2 Timothy 3:16–17 (NSV) points in this direction. Scripture equips believers for every good work. That does not mean it answers every curiosity. It means it provides what is necessary to live faithfully.

Across church history, this principle has guarded the church from two dangers:

- **Adding to Scripture** as if God's Word is incomplete.
- **Replacing Scripture** with personal experiences or traditions as final authority.

Tradition can be helpful. Church history can clarify. Teachers can guide. But none of these can take the place of Scripture's final authority.

5) Grasp Clarity: Scripture Is Understandable in Its Main Message

Some people avoid the Bible because they assume it is too hard. Others avoid it because they want to keep control. The doctrine of clarity confronts both.

Clarity does not mean every passage is equally plain. It means the Bible's main message is clear enough for ordinary believers, using normal means, to understand what God requires for salvation and faithful living.

Psalm 119:105 (NSV) describes God's word as a lamp to the feet and a light to the path. A lamp does not show you everything at once. It shows you enough to take the next faithful step. That is the Bible's practical clarity.

The New Testament assumes believers can read and understand Scripture. Paul's letters were read to whole churches, including people with different levels of education. He expects them to learn, apply, and grow.

Clarity also means Scripture interprets Scripture. When you are confused by one passage, you look for other passages that speak more directly. Over time, the Bible becomes its own teacher.

6) Use Sound Reading Habits: Context, Genre, and Repetition

Clarity becomes real in your life when you adopt good habits.

Read in context.

Ask: Who is speaking? To whom? What problem is being addressed? What comes before and after?

Recognize genre.

Poetry uses imagery. Proverbs give general patterns, not guaranteed outcomes in every case. Narratives describe events, but not every event is a command. Letters contain direct instruction for church life.

Notice repetition.

Scripture repeats key truths. God's holiness is repeated. Human sin is repeated. God's promise to save is repeated. Christ's resurrection is repeated. Repetition signals emphasis.

Summarize in your own words.

After reading a section, state the main point in one sentence. This simple practice exposes misunderstandings early.

7) Learn How the Church Has Protected Scripture's Authority

Throughout history, the church has faced pressure to lower Scripture's status. Sometimes the pressure comes from government power. Sometimes from intellectual fashion. Sometimes from church leaders who want to control people.

During the Protestant Reformation, one major emphasis was that Scripture is the final standard for doctrine and practice. The church did not reject all tradition. It rejected tradition as the highest authority. That debate still matters because many believers today feel pulled between

Scripture and strong voices—online teachers, political movements, or popular therapy language.

The church's enduring need is the same: receive God's Word as God's Word.

You will meet common objections. Many are sincere questions. Some are excuses. Either way, you should learn to respond calmly.

"There are many interpretations, so we cannot know what Scripture means."

There are many interpretations because humans disagree, not because Scripture is meaningless. On central matters—God's nature, sin, Christ, salvation, holiness—Scripture is clear. Disagreements often arise from ignoring context or forcing the text to serve an agenda.

"The Bible was written long ago, so it cannot address modern life."

Scripture addresses the heart, and the heart has not changed. Technologies change, but pride, fear, lust, greed, bitterness, and unbelief remain. Scripture speaks to the roots. Wise application brings it into present situations.

"My experience feels more real than what I read."

Experiences are powerful, but they are not final. Scripture corrects experiences and interprets them. If you let experience overrule Scripture, you will drift into confusion.

9) Put Scripture's Authority into Practice

Here is where this chapter becomes personal. Many people claim the Bible is authoritative. Few let it correct them.

Scripture's authority shows up in three measurable ways:

1. **Your willingness to obey when it is costly.**
2. **Your willingness to change your mind when Scripture corrects you.**
3. **Your willingness to submit desires to God rather than bending God to desires.**

Jesus compares obedience to building on rock (Matthew 7:24–27, NSV). The storm reveals the foundation. It is easy to claim authority during calm days. It is harder when obedience brings tension, loss, or ridicule.

A steady Christian learns to obey Scripture before the storm arrives.

10) Read the Bible as a Means of Grace

The Bible is not only a source of doctrine. It is a means God uses to strengthen faith. When you read Scripture, you are not merely gathering data. You are meeting God through His Word.

That does not mean every reading session feels warm. Some sessions feel dry. Some confront sin. Some expose confusion. Keep going. Over time, Scripture shapes instincts. It reforms priorities. It rebuilds hope.

To keep it simple, use this weekly pattern:

- **Daily:** read one chapter and write a one-sentence summary.
- **Weekly:** choose one key passage to memorize.
- **Ongoing:** bring your questions to a local church, not only to the internet.

Scripture was not given to isolate you. It was given to form you within God's people.

CHAPTER 5

RELY ON GOD'S PROVIDENCE: SEE HIS RULE OVER NATURE, NATIONS, AND DAILY LIFE

Most believers say, "God is in control," until life stops feeling controlled. A diagnosis arrives. A job ends. A child wanders. A conflict hardens. In those moments, the doctrine of providence moves from a word you recognize to a truth you must lean on.

This chapter will help you rely on providence with clarity. We will define it, show it in Scripture, address common misunderstandings, and apply it to fear, suffering, planning, and prayer.

1) Define Providence in Plain Words

Providence includes three inseparable truths:

1. **God preserves**: He sustains the world and every creature moment by moment.
2. **God governs**: He rules events, choices, and outcomes without losing control.
3. **God provides**: He cares for His people with wise fatherly care.

A key text is Psalm 103:19 (NSV): the Lord has established His throne in the heavens, and His kingdom rules over all. That is comprehensive. Nothing sits outside His royal authority.

Another key text is Ephesians 1:11 (NSV): God works all things according to the counsel of His will. Scripture does not say God reacts to history. It says God works within history to accomplish His purpose.

Providence is not fate. Fate is impersonal. Providence is personal rule by the living God. Providence also is not a vague optimism. It is the conviction that God is present and active in every season.

2) Hold Together God's Rule and Human Responsibility

A common worry appears quickly. If God rules all things, do human choices matter? Yes, because Scripture affirms both God's sovereignty and real human responsibility.

Proverbs 16:9 (NSV) says the heart of a man plans his way, but the Lord establishes his steps. That verse does not cancel planning. It places planning under God's rule. Humans make meaningful choices. God governs outcomes.

Here is the point you must keep: God's providence does not turn people into puppets. Scripture treats human decisions as morally significant and accountable. At the same time, Scripture refuses to place God at the mercy of human will.

This balance protects you from two opposite errors:

- **Passive fatalism**: "Nothing I do matters, so I will do nothing."
- **Anxious control**: "Everything depends on me, so I must manage everything."

Providence produces a third posture: **responsible action with settled trust**.

3) See Providence in Creation and Daily Provision

Jesus points to small details to teach big trust. In Matthew 10:29–31 (NSV), He speaks about sparrows that do not fall apart from the Father's care, then He says you are worth more than many sparrows. The argument is simple: if God attends to small creatures, He does not ignore His children.

That passage does not promise comfort at every moment. It promises attention. God's care is not distant. It is direct.

Acts 17:26–28 (NSV) adds another layer. Paul tells the Athenians that God determined times and boundaries for nations, and that in Him we live and move and have our being. Providence covers biology, geography, history, and breath. God is not locked inside religious spaces. He rules the ordinary world.

This means your daily life is not spiritually empty. Meals, work, schedules, setbacks, and relationships all sit under God's rule. The Christian does not divide life into "God's territory" and "real life." All of life is lived before God.

4) Learn How Providence Works in Suffering

Providence becomes hardest when you face pain. You may be tempted to choose between two bad options: either God is good but weak, or God is strong but harsh. Scripture rejects that false choice. God is both sovereign and good.

Romans 8:28 (NSV) is one of the clearest statements: God works all things for good for those who love Him and are called according to His purpose. The verse does not say all things are good. It says God works in all things for good. That difference matters.

What does "good" mean in that verse? The context points to being conformed to the image of Christ (Romans 8:29, NSV). God's goal is not short-term comfort. God's goal is Christlike maturity, steadfast faith, and final glory.

Does this make suffering easy to bear? No, but it prevents despair. It anchors suffering in a purposeful story rather than chaos.

Church history reflects this same conviction. Augustine wrote often about God's rule even in a broken world, insisting that evil is never equal to God. Centuries later, many Reformers emphasized providence not to produce cold theory, but to provide comfort in unstable times. The point was pastoral: believers can rest because the Father reigns.

Many confessions echo that pastoral aim. They speak of providence as God's fatherly hand that governs all things for the good of His people. That language has helped generations stand firm in persecution, illness, poverty, and uncertainty.

5) Use Joseph's Story as a Case Study

Genesis 50:20 (NSV) gives one of the clearest windows into providence in human history. Joseph speaks to the brothers who betrayed him. He says they meant evil against him, but God meant it for good, to preserve many lives.

Notice what the verse does and does not do.

- It **does** call their action evil. Providence does not rename sin as virtue.
- It **does** say God had a good purpose that overruled their evil intent.

- It **does not** say God excused their guilt.
- It **does not** remove Joseph's pain or deny his years of hardship.

This is providence with moral clarity. Humans can intend evil. God can intend good through the same event without being the author of sin. Scripture is comfortable saying both.

If you want a mature view of providence, return to Joseph often. It teaches patience. It teaches forgiveness without pretending. It teaches that God can bring life out of what looked like ruin.

6) Avoid Common Distortions of Providence

Distortion 1: "Everything That Happens Must Be Good"

This sounds pious, but it is careless. Scripture calls many things evil: oppression, deceit, violence, abuse. To call evil "good" is to mis-speak. It can also harm the wounded.

A better statement is this: **God is good, and God can work good through evil without approving evil.**

Distortion 2: "Providence Means I Do Not Need Wisdom"

Some believers stop planning and stop seeking counsel. Scripture never teaches that. Proverbs is filled with calls to wisdom, diligence, and restraint. Providence does not cancel means. God often provides through ordinary means: work, medicine, wise counsel, and faithful planning.

Distortion 3: "Providence Means God Does Not Care About My Tears"

Providence can be misused as a cold answer: "God is sovereign, so stop crying." That is not biblical. Scripture includes lament and grief. Jesus Himself wept. God's rule does not erase sorrow. It gives sorrow a place to go.

Here is the question many people fear to ask: *If God rules, why pray?* Because God ordains both the ends and the means, and prayer is one of His appointed means. Scripture presents prayer as real participation in God's work. You do not pray to inform God. You pray to honor God, ask for help, and align your will with His.

7) Apply Providence to Planning and Decision-Making

Providence gives you a stable approach to choices.

1. **Use wisdom**: gather facts, seek counsel, and consider consequences.
2. **Obey Scripture**: never choose what God forbids, even if it seems efficient.
3. **Act with humility**: make plans, then hold them loosely.
4. **Trust God with outcomes**: do your duty, and leave the result to God.

This does not remove tension. It removes panic. It also guards you from interpreting every closed door as punishment or every open door as approval. Doors open for many reasons. You need Scripture, wisdom, and prayer to interpret them.

A steady life does not require perfect foresight. It requires faithful steps under God's care.

8) Let Providence Produce Four Practical Fruits

Fruit 1: Courage

If God reigns, you can obey even when obedience costs you. Fear loses some of its power when you remember God's throne is not threatened.

Fruit 2: Patience

Providence teaches timing. God often works slowly. He forms character over years, not days. You may not see what He is doing right now, but His work continues.

Fruit 3: Gratitude

Every ordinary good becomes a gift. Food, sleep, friendship, and work are no longer "normal." They are provision from the Father's hand.

Fruit 4: Repentance and Humility

Providence confronts pride. You are not the center. You are not in charge. This is not crushing; it is freeing. You are a creature loved by the Creator.

9) Practice a Simple Providence Prayer

Use a short pattern that joins trust and action:

1. **Name what you control** (choices, obedience, attitude).

2. **Name what you do not control** (timing, outcomes, other people).

3. **Ask for wisdom and courage** for what you must do.

4. **Entrust outcomes to God** and choose one next faithful step.

This is not a formula. It is a way to pray like a Christian who believes God reigns and listens.

Providence is not meant to satisfy curiosity. It is meant to steady the soul. The Lord's throne stands. His care reaches into your day. So you can plan, obey, repent, work, and rest without living as if the world depends on you.

CHAPTER 6

WORSHIP GOD AS CREATOR: CONNECT CREATION, ORDER, AND HUMAN PURPOSE

Many people treat creation as background scenery. Scripture treats it as testimony. The Bible begins with God creating, not because God needed a world, but because God chose to make one. Creation reveals God's power, wisdom, generosity, and authority. It also tells you something about yourself: you are not self-made, and you are not accidental. You were made by God and for God.

This chapter will help you worship God as Creator in a way that shapes daily life. We will look at what Scripture teaches about creation, why order matters, what it means to be made in God's image, and how creation connects to work, rest, and responsibility. We will also address common confusions that weaken faith.

1) Begin with the Bible's Opening Claim: God Created All Things

Genesis 1:1 (NSV) is direct: "In the beginning God created the heavens and the earth." The verse is not an argument. It is a declaration. Scripture does not introduce God as a discovery. It introduces God as the Creator who already exists.

This single statement sets a clear boundary against two errors:

- The world is not divine. God is not part of the world. God made the world.

- The world is not ultimate. The created order has purpose because it came from a purposeful Maker.

When Christians confess God as Creator, we confess His rightful ownership. Creation belongs to God. Life belongs to God. You belong to God.

2) Learn What Creation Shows About God

Scripture repeatedly links creation to God's glory and power.

Psalm 33:6–9 (NSV) emphasizes God's effective speech: He spoke, and it came to be. This is not a poetic exaggeration. It is the Bible's way of saying God creates with authority. He does not struggle. He does not compete with another power. He commands, and reality responds.

Jeremiah 10:12 (NSV) highlights God's wisdom: He made the earth by His power and established the world by His wisdom. Creation is not random assembly. It reflects design, order, and purposeful arrangement.

These texts do not answer every modern question about processes and timelines. Their primary aim is theological: the world is God's work, so the world is meaningful.

Practical result: worship begins with recognition. You are living in God's world, not your own. That changes the way you treat people, time, money, and the earth itself.

3) Understand Order: God Made a World You Can Live In

Creation is not chaos. God forms and fills. He separates light from darkness, land from seas, and then places living creatures in their proper domains. The repeated pattern in Genesis 1 is "and it was so." God's word brings stability.

Order is not a cage. Order is a gift. It makes life possible. It supports learning, work, community, and stewardship. When Scripture speaks about God's providence and wisdom, it often assumes this ordered creation.

This also connects to moral order. Many people today want the benefits of an ordered world but reject a moral order that comes from God. Scripture ties them together. If God is Creator, then God defines the good. The created world is not a blank canvas for self-definition. It is a world with a Maker, and a Maker's purposes.

Practical result: you can submit to God's design with trust rather than suspicion. God's commands are not random restrictions. They flow from His wisdom as Creator.

4) Receive the Gift of Being Human: Made in God's Image

Genesis 1:26–27 (NSV) teaches that God made humanity in His image. This does not mean humans are divine. It means humans reflect God in a creaturely way. We can know, love, rule responsibly, communicate, create, and live in moral relationship.

The image of God is foundational for human dignity. It applies to every human being, not only the strong, the young, the healthy, or the useful. The unborn, the elderly, the disabled, the poor, and the outsider all bear God's image. That is why Scripture condemns violence and contempt. Human life is sacred because it is God-given.

This truth also corrects pride. Being in God's image does not mean you are the center. It means you are accountable to the One you reflect. Image implies representation. You are meant to live in a way that points beyond yourself.

Practical result: treat people as image-bearers. Speak with care. Refuse cruelty. Practice honesty. Protect the vulnerable. These are not optional ethics. They are consequences of creation.

5) Connect Creation to Calling: Work and Stewardship

Work is not a punishment. Work appears before the fall. Genesis 2:15 (NSV) says God placed the man in the garden to work it and keep it. That means work is part of God's good design. Work is one way humans reflect God's wise rule.

This changes how you view ordinary labor. Work is not only about income. Work is a calling to serve others and honor God. Some work is public; some is hidden. Both matter. A parent caring for children, a mechanic repairing engines, a nurse tending wounds, and a teacher shaping minds are all serving within God's created order.

Stewardship follows naturally. To "keep" the garden implies responsibility. The earth is not a god to worship. It is not a toy to abuse. It is God's possession entrusted to human care.

Church history often emphasized this connection. Many Christian teachers spoke about vocation as service. The value of work was tied to God's creation design, not only to personal ambition.

Practical result: ask a simple question about your labor: "Who does this serve?" When your work serves people and honors God's commands, it becomes an act of worship.

6) Receive Rest as a Created Good: The Pattern of Sabbath

Genesis 2:2–3 (NSV) teaches that God rested on the seventh day and blessed it. God did not rest because He was tired. God rested to set a pattern. Rest declares that the world does not depend on your constant activity.

Rest is both spiritual and practical. It trains you to trust God's providence. It also protects you from burnout and from the pride that assumes your work holds the world together.

The Bible's later teaching about Sabbath is rich and sometimes debated across traditions. Christians differ on how Sabbath observance applies under the new covenant. Yet the core principle remains: God builds rest into faithful living. Jesus also calls the weary to come to Him for rest (Matthew 11:28–29, NSV). That rest is not only a schedule. It is a relationship with the Lord who carries burdens.

Practical result: plan rest. Treat it as obedience, not laziness. Make space for worship, family, and renewal. Your limits are not failures. They are part of creaturehood.

7) Face the Fall without Losing the Goodness of Creation

Genesis teaches creation is good, and it also teaches creation is now broken by sin. The fall affects human hearts, relationships, work, and the wider world. Yet Scripture never treats creation as worthless. It treats creation as damaged and groaning, awaiting renewal.

Romans 8:19–22 (NSV) speaks of creation's longing for liberation from corruption. That passage is not merely poetic. It frames history. God will not discard His world. He will redeem it. That connects creation to the future hope we will study later.

This guards you from two errors:

- **Despising the material world** as if spirituality means escape from creation.
- **Worshiping the material world** as if creation is the highest good.

Christian faith refuses both. The Creator is to be worshiped. Creation is to be stewarded and enjoyed with gratitude.

Practical result: enjoy created goods without making them ultimate. Food, art, music, nature, and friendship are gifts. Receive them with thanks. Do not treat them as saviors.

8) Answer Common Confusions with Calm Clarity

Confusion 1: "Science and Scripture must be enemies."

Scripture and honest observation of the world need not be enemies because God is the author of both creation and revelation. Many historical Christians worked in science precisely because they believed the world is ordered and intelligible.

Still, Scripture's purpose is not to be a modern textbook. Its purpose is to reveal God and His saving plan. So you should not force Scripture into questions it was not written to answer. At the same time, you should not let modern theories erase what Scripture clearly teaches: God is Creator, and humans are His creatures.

Confusion 2: "If God made the world, then the world is perfect as it is."

No. Scripture teaches the fall. The world contains beauty and disorder, pleasure and pain. Creation points to God's goodness, but it also shows the need for redemption.

Confusion 3: "Purpose is self-chosen."

Scripture teaches purpose is received from God. That does not erase creativity or personal calling. It anchors them. You are free to choose many paths, but you are not free to redefine the good apart from the Creator.

9) Let Creation Theology Shape Everyday Ethics

If God is Creator, then certain ethical conclusions follow.

- **Human life has dignity** because God gives it and images Himself in it.
- **Sex and marriage have meaning** because God designs bodies and covenant life.

- **Truth matters** because God is truthful and made humans to communicate.
- **Justice matters** because God rules the world in righteousness.

This does not make Christian ethics simplistic. It makes them grounded. You do not build morality on shifting trends. You build it on creation order and God's revealed will.

10) Practice One Week of "Creator-Focused" Living

Try a simple practice for seven days.

1. Each morning, read one Psalm that praises God as Creator.
2. Each day, thank God for three created gifts (food, air, sunlight, friendship, skill).
3. Choose one act of stewardship: care for a person, care for a space, or care for a task you usually neglect.
4. End each day with one sentence: "I am a creature, and God is faithful."

This is not sentimental. It is honest. It places you back in reality.

God is Creator. You are His creature. That is not a limitation. It is a gift. It means you can worship, work, rest, and hope with purpose.

BOOK TWO
UNDERSTAND HUMANITY UNDER GOD

A Simple Guide to the Image of God, Sin, Conscience, and Community

CHAPTER 1

ACCEPT HUMAN WORTH: LEARN WHAT "IMAGE OF GOD" MEANS FOR DAILY LIFE

People swing between two bad stories about humanity. One story says humans are basically good, so we only need encouragement. The other story says humans are basically worthless, so we should expect little more than selfishness. Scripture refuses both. The Bible teaches real dignity and real ruin at the same time. If you miss either side, you will harm people and confuse the gospel.

This chapter focuses on human worth. That may sound obvious, but it is not. Many Christians carry quiet contempt for themselves, while others carry loud contempt for their neighbors. Both errors grow in the same soil: forgetting what God says about human life. When you accept human worth as Scripture defines it, you gain a steadier view of yourself and others. You also gain a clearer reason to love, protect, and speak truth.

1) Begin with the Source of Human Worth

Human worth does not start with talent, health, strength, age, or productivity. It starts with God's act of creation and God's claim over His creatures. Scripture grounds dignity in God's design, not in social approval.

Psalm 8:4–6 (NSV) captures the wonder well. The writer looks at the vast heavens and asks why God is mindful of man. Then he states the answer: God crowned humanity with glory and honor and appointed humans to a responsible role in His world. The point is not that humans are great by nature. The point is that God gives a gifted status and a calling.

This means your worth is not fragile. It does not rise and fall with mood, income, or appearance. It rests on God's decision to create and honor human life.

2) Learn What the "Image of God" Includes

The Bible teaches that humans are made in God's image. Even when you do not quote the first chapter of Genesis, Scripture keeps returning to that truth in other places and builds ethical conclusions from it.

Genesis 9:6 (NSV) treats human life as uniquely protected because humans bear God's image. That passage appears after the flood, in a fallen world. It shows that the image is still a moral reality after sin entered the human story. Human dignity is not erased by human failure.

So what does "image of God" mean in daily terms?

It means humans are personal.

We are not only biological organisms. We think, choose, communicate, and form moral relationships.

It means humans are moral.

We are accountable. We can do right and wrong. We can repent. We can grow in wisdom.

It means humans are relational.

We are built for family, community, and covenant. Isolation damages us.

It means humans are responsible.

We can steward, build, organize, and serve. We are meant to cultivate and protect.

It means humans can reflect God.

We do not share God's essence, but we can display His character in a creaturely way: truthfulness, justice, mercy, creativity, and love.

Does this mean every person reflects God equally well at all times? No, because sin distorts the image's expression. Yet the image remains the basis for dignity and the reason Scripture condemns contempt.

3) Treat Speech as a Test of Your View of Human Worth

Scripture ties the image of God directly to how you talk about people.

James 3:9–10 (NSV) warns that with the tongue we bless the Lord, and with the same tongue we curse people who are made in God's likeness. James treats this as a moral contradiction. He does not excuse it as a personality trait. He names it as spiritual disorder.

This matters because speech is where contempt often hides. People may never throw a punch, yet they strike with words. They mock weakness. They reduce people to labels. They spread rumors. They talk about others as if they are objects.

If you accept the image of God, your speech must change. You can still confront sin. You can still tell hard truths. But you cannot treat image-bearers as disposable.

A simple practice helps: before you speak about someone, ask what your words are trying to accomplish. Are you aiming to build, correct, protect, or heal? Or are you trying to dominate, shame, and win?

4) Hold Dignity and Difference Together

Scripture teaches equal worth, and it also teaches real difference. God made humans male and female. God gives different gifts. God assigns different roles in families and communities. Yet those differences never cancel dignity.

In Galatians 3:28 (NSV), Paul insists that in Christ there is no hierarchy of worth based on ethnicity, social status, or sex. The verse does not erase all distinctions in life. It does erase any claim that some people are closer to God by nature and others are second-class.

This truth matters for churches and families. It calls leaders to lead with honor. It calls parents to treat children as persons, not projects. It calls husbands and wives to serve one another with respect. It calls believers to welcome the poor, the outsider, and the wounded, not as charity cases, but as neighbors.

The image of God becomes clearer when you see Jesus. Scripture calls Christ the visible image of the invisible God (Colossians 1:15, NSV). Jesus shows what true humanity looks like under God: obedient, truthful, compassionate, strong, and clean.

This protects you from another common error. Many people measure human worth by performance. Scripture measures human worth by creation and then shows restored humanity in Christ. Jesus is not only the Savior from sin. He is also the model of faithful human life.

When you look at Christ, you see dignity without pride and humility without self-hatred. You see authority used for service. You see strength paired with gentleness. That is what God aims to form in His people.

6) Apply Human Worth to the Hard Places

The doctrine of the image of God is not only for debates. It is for the hardest places in life: conflict, weakness, aging, and suffering.

When you face weakness in yourself:

You do not need to despise yourself to grow. You can repent without self-hatred. You can seek help without shame. Worth and weakness can exist in the same person, because worth rests on God's gift, not your power.

When you face weakness in others:

You do not treat people as burdens. You treat them as neighbors. This includes those who cannot "pay you back." It includes the sick, the elderly, and the disabled. The image of God calls for patient honor.

When you face conflict:

You can confront wrong without dehumanizing the person who did it. That does not mean you ignore harm. It means you pursue justice without contempt.

When you face cultural pressure to reduce people to categories:

You resist. Scripture gives you a better lens. You see persons, not stereotypes. You see souls, not talking points.

Is it naïve to treat everyone as an image-bearer in a harsh world? No, because Scripture does not deny evil. It commands love in the presence of evil. It also gives tools for protection, boundaries, and accountability.

7) Watch for Two Dangers: Pride and Despair

The image of God guards you from despair, but it can be twisted into pride.

Pride says: "I am made in God's image, so I answer to no one."

Scripture rejects that. The image includes accountability. You are a representative under the King, not a rival to the King.

Despair says: "I am too broken to matter."

Scripture rejects that too. Even in a fallen world, the image remains the basis for dignity and the reason God calls for mercy and justice.

A balanced view says: "I matter because God made me. I must repent because I have sinned. I have hope because God restores."

8) Practice Honor as a Daily Discipline

Honor is not flattery. Honor means you treat people as weighty because God made them. It changes habits.

- You listen without interrupting.
- You tell the truth without cruelty.
- You keep promises because your word affects image-bearers.
- You refuse gossip because it tears down.
- You protect the vulnerable because God does.

Honor also shapes how you view your own body and life. Your body is not an accident. Your life is not your own possession. This will matter later when we discuss sin, conscience, and the moral life. For now, receive a basic truth: being human is a gift before it is a problem.

9) Bring It into the Church: A Community of Honor

The church should be the safest place to be treated as a person. That does not mean the church is perfect. It means the church should aim for a culture shaped by the image of God.

This includes practical commitments:

- Take repentance seriously, because sin harms people.
- Take forgiveness seriously, because grace restores people.
- Take discipline seriously, because love protects people.
- Take service seriously, because Christ dignifies people.

When a church forgets human worth, it becomes harsh or shallow. When a church remembers human worth, it becomes a place where truth and mercy can meet.

10) Summarize the Point You Must Keep

Human worth is not earned. It is received from God. The image of God explains why human life is sacred, why speech matters, why justice matters, and why love is commanded. It also prepares you for the next chapters, because the same Bible that gives dignity also explains what went wrong in the human heart.

You can accept human worth without denying human sin. In fact, you must hold both, or you will either excuse evil or crush the wounded. Scripture calls you to a stronger path: honor people as God's creatures, and call people back to God's ways.

CHAPTER 2

FACE THE FALL HONESTLY: TRACE HOW SIN ENTERED AND SPREAD

If you only believe in human worth, you will not understand the world you live in. You will be confused by betrayal, addiction, violence, and hypocrisy—especially in yourself. Scripture honors human dignity, but it also tells the truth about human ruin. The Bible calls that ruin "sin," and it traces sin to a decisive turning point: the fall.

The fall is not a minor detail. It explains why people who know better still do wrong. It explains why good gifts become idols. It explains why shame and blame are so common. It also explains why salvation must be rescue, not self-improvement.

This chapter will trace how sin entered and spread, using Scripture's storyline and the church's careful reflection across history. We will look at the first transgression, the nature of temptation, the results of sin, and the way sin multiplies in families and nations. We will also address common modern misunderstandings that soften sin into mere weakness.

1) Start with God's Good World and a Clear Command

Genesis begins with a good creation. God speaks, orders, blesses, and calls His work good. Humanity is placed in a garden not as prisoners, but as stewards. In that setting, God gives a command.

Genesis 2:16–17 (NSV) records it: God permits wide freedom—every tree except one. The boundary is clear, reasonable, and relational. The command also includes a warning: disobedience leads to death.

This matters because the fall did not come from scarcity. It came from abundance. Sin entered not because God withheld good, but because humans distrusted God's goodness and wanted autonomy.

Modern people often assume rules are signs of oppression. Scripture presents God's command as wise love. The boundary was meant to protect life and preserve trust.

2) Watch How Temptation Works: The Lie Attacks God's Character

Genesis 3 shows the strategy of temptation with frightening clarity. The serpent does not begin by denying God's existence. He begins by questioning God's word.

In Genesis 3:1 (NSV), the serpent twists God's command: "Did God really say...?" The goal is to plant suspicion. Then the serpent escalates: he denies the consequence and promises a different outcome.

The lie attacks three areas:

1. **God's word**: "Did God really say?"
2.
3. **God's justice**: "You will not surely die."
4. **God's goodness**: "God knows ... you will be like God."

Temptation often follows this pattern today. It does not always present itself as rebellion. It presents itself as freedom. It suggests God is holding you back. It suggests obedience is naïve. It suggests you deserve more control.

Notice also how the lie makes sin look small and God's warning look exaggerated. That is a common move. Sin often enters the heart when you minimize consequences and maximize your own right to choose.

3) Identify the Heart of Sin: Self-Rule

At its core, sin is not only breaking a rule. It is turning from God to self-rule. It is choosing independence over trust.

Genesis 3:6 (NSV) describes the act: the woman sees, desires, takes, and eats; then she gives to her husband, and he eats. The language is simple, and that is part of its power. The moment is not described with drama. It is described like ordinary choice. Sin often begins as an ordinary choice that says, "My desire outranks God's word."

Church history has often described this as pride and disordered love. Augustine argued that sin is love turned inward, where the self becomes the center. That is not academic language. It is practical. When the self becomes the center, everything else becomes a tool: people, work, sex, money, even religion.

This also explains why sin spreads. Self-centeredness does not remain private. It shapes relationships.

As soon as Adam and Eve sin, the story shifts.

Genesis 3:7–10 (NSV) shows shame. They realize they are naked and hide. Shame is not only embarrassment. It is the sense of exposure and vulnerability before God and others. They cover themselves, and they avoid God's presence.

Then comes blame. Genesis 3:12–13 (NSV) shows each person shifting responsibility. Adam blames the woman and, indirectly, God: "the woman You gave me." The woman blames the serpent. Sin quickly turns people into self-defenders.

Then comes separation. The relationship with God becomes strained. The relationship between man and woman becomes strained. Harmony breaks. The fall fractures communion.

These results matter because they still describe life today. People hide. People cover. People blame. People avoid responsibility. People avoid God.

If you want to understand your own habits, ask where you hide, where you blame, and where you refuse honesty.

Genesis 3 includes judgment, and it also includes mercy.

God's judgment is real. The serpent is cursed. The woman's pain and conflict are increased. The man's work becomes hard and resisting. Death enters the human story. God's warning was not empty.

Yet God's mercy appears in several ways.

First, God seeks them. He asks, "Where are you?" (Genesis 3:9, NSV). That is not a request for information. It is a summons to confession.

Second, God provides clothing. Genesis 3:21 (NSV) says God made garments for them and clothed them. Their fig leaves were inadequate. God covers their shame more effectively than they can cover themselves.

Third, God gives a promise. Genesis 3:15 (NSV) speaks of the offspring who will crush the serpent's head. This is the first hint of redemption. The promise is not full detail, but it is a direction: God will act to defeat evil and restore what sin ruined.

This is important for the whole Bible. From the start, God's response to sin includes both judgment and a saving promise. The story does not end in the garden. It moves toward the cross.

6) Follow the Spread of Sin: From One Act to a Flood

Sin does not remain contained. Genesis quickly shows sin multiplying.

Genesis 4 records the first murder. Cain kills Abel. Then Cain denies responsibility: "Am I my brother's keeper?" (Genesis 4:9, NSV). That question captures the fall's logic. Self-rule refuses responsibility for others.

Soon, violence becomes normal. By Genesis 6:5 (NSV), Scripture says the intent of human hearts was continually evil. That statement is sweeping. It describes a moral collapse, not merely isolated mistakes.

The flood narrative is one of Scripture's clearest witnesses that sin is not a small flaw. It corrupts human society. It spreads across generations. It turns culture into a machine for producing harm.

At the same time, Genesis also shows God preserving a line of promise. God keeps His saving purpose moving forward.

7) Learn the Doctrines of "Original Sin" and "Sin's Spread" with Care

The church has used the term "original sin" to describe two related truths:

1. The first sin was the origin point of human rebellion.
2. Human beings now inherit a sinful condition that inclines them toward sin.

You do not need to use the term "original sin" to believe the biblical teaching. But it is useful language because it summarizes what Scripture shows.

Romans 5:12 (NSV) teaches that sin came into the world through one man, and death through sin, and so death spread to all because all sinned. This passage is important because it links Adam's sin to the universal reality of death and sin.

The point is not that humans are forced to sin against their will. The point is that human nature after the fall is bent. We sin because we are sinners, and we are sinners because the human race is now fallen.

Church history debated details of how Adam's sin relates to all humanity, but the central agreement has been strong: sin is universal, deep, and inherited in the sense that all humans are born into a corrupted condition.

This explains why sin appears early in life without needing to be taught. Children do not need lessons in selfishness. They need training in patience and truth. The bent is already present.

8) Face Total Corruption without Despair

Christians have sometimes used the phrase "total depravity." Many misunderstand it. It does not mean every person is as evil as possible. It means sin affects every part of the person: mind, will, desires, and actions.

Ephesians 2:1–3 (NSV) describes people apart from Christ as dead in trespasses, following sinful desires, and by nature children of wrath. That is strong language. It tells you sin is not merely an external habit. It is a spiritual condition.

Yet Scripture also teaches that humans still bear God's image. That means fallen humans can still do acts of kindness, create beauty, and build societies. The problem is that sin distorts motives and aims. Even good deeds can be done for pride, control, or fear. Without God, even "good" can become a path away from God.

Facing this truth should not produce despair. It should produce humility and hope. Humility, because you cannot fix yourself. Hope, because God's salvation is a real rescue.

9) Reject Modern Softening of Sin

Modern culture often avoids moral language. It prefers categories like "mistakes," "brokenness," or "struggle." Those words can describe real pain, but they can also hide guilt.

Scripture speaks more directly. Sin is lawlessness, rebellion, and unbelief. It is refusing God's rightful rule.

Why does this matter? Because you cannot repent of what you will not name. If sin is merely weakness, then you only need support. If sin is guilt before God, then you need forgiveness and change.

The gospel offers both comfort and correction. But it begins with truth.

10) Put the Fall into Your Own Story

The fall is not only a past event. It describes what happens in every human heart when temptation arrives.

The pattern still holds:

- Question God's word.
- Doubt God's goodness.
- Desire control.
- Take what is forbidden.
- Hide, blame, and harden.

If you can see that pattern in your own life, you can interrupt it earlier. You can respond to temptation with confession, Scripture, and prayer before sin grows.

And here is the hope: the story does not end with Adam. Scripture presents Christ as the one who obeys where Adam failed. Later we will study salvation in depth. For now, the truth is simple: the fall explains what is wrong, and God's promise points to what He will do to make things right.

CHAPTER 3

RECOGNIZE SIN'S PATTERNS: NAME PRIDE, IDOLATRY, AND SELF - RULE

Sin rarely announces itself with a warning label. It usually arrives as a pattern, a habit, a reflex. It feels normal because it has been practiced. That is one reason Scripture speaks so often about watchfulness. If you can learn to recognize sin's patterns, you can repent earlier, seek help sooner, and avoid damage that spreads into your relationships.

This chapter will name three core patterns Scripture exposes again and again: **pride**, **idolatry**, and **self-rule**. These patterns overlap. They often appear together. When you learn to spot them, you gain a clearer view of your own heart, and you gain a steadier way to counsel and care for others.

1) Start with the Heart: Sin Grows from the Inside Out

Many people treat sin as a behavior problem. Scripture goes deeper. The Bible treats sin as a heart problem that produces behaviors.

Jeremiah 17:9 (NSV) gives a sober assessment: the heart is deceitful above all things and desperately sick; who can understand it? The verse does not mean you cannot know anything about yourself. It means your inner life can mislead you. You can excuse what is harmful. You can call darkness "light" when you want control.

This is why biblical repentance starts with honesty before God. You do not merely stop a habit. You expose the desires and beliefs that feed it. Then you bring those desires under God's authority.

If that sounds discouraging, remember the purpose of the diagnosis. God exposes the heart so He can heal the heart. Scripture does not reveal sin to shame you into paralysis. It reveals sin so you can be freed from its grip.

2) Name Pride: The Desire to Rise, Control, and Be Seen

Pride is not limited to arrogance and loud self-praise. Pride is any posture that places the self above God and above others. Pride wants to be central. Pride wants to be uncorrectable. Pride wants the final word.

Proverbs 16:18 (NSV) warns that pride goes before destruction, and a haughty spirit before a fall. This is not superstition. It is moral cause and effect. Pride makes you careless. It makes you overconfident. It makes you slow to listen. Then it sets you up for collapse.

Pride also hides under respectable forms:

- **Spiritual pride**: "God is fortunate to have me."
- **Intellectual pride**: "If I understand it, it must be true."
- **Moral pride**: "My sins are smaller than theirs."
- **Victim pride**: "Because I suffered, I can do as I please."
- **Quiet pride**: "I will never ask for help; I will prove myself."

In church history, Augustine wrote at length about pride as a root sin. He described it as the soul turned in on itself. That phrase matters because pride is not only self-love. Pride is self as the reference point for everything. God becomes a tool. People become props. Even good deeds become trophies.

How do you identify pride in daily life? Look for defensiveness when corrected. Look for joy when others fail. Look for resentment when someone else receives honor. Pride reveals itself by how it reacts, not only by what it says.

3) Name Idolatry: When Good Gifts Become False Gods

Idolatry sounds like a problem from the ancient world: statues, temples, and rituals. Scripture teaches a wider meaning. An idol is anything you trust, fear, or love more than God.

Ezekiel 14:3 (NSV) describes "idols in the heart." That phrase is crucial. Idolatry can exist without a statue. It can live in motives, longings, and private loyalties.

Idols often begin as good gifts:

- Work becomes identity.
- Family becomes ultimate.
- Romance becomes salvation.

- Money becomes security.
- Comfort becomes the highest goal.
- Reputation becomes a god you must feed.

Paul makes this concrete when he speaks of greed as idolatry (Colossians 3:5, NSV). Greed is not only wanting more. It is trusting more. It is treating possessions as protection and meaning.

Idolatry also explains why sin can feel necessary. If your idol is approval, then lying feels necessary. If your idol is control, then anger feels justified. If your idol is comfort, then compromise feels reasonable.

Martin Luther often said the human heart functions like an idol factory. His point was practical: if you tear one idol down, you will likely try to build another. That is why repentance is not a one-time event. It is a pattern of turning from false gods to the true God.

4) Name Self-Rule: The Refusal to Be Ruled by God

Self-rule is the engine behind pride and idolatry. It is the quiet decision: "I will decide what is right for me." Scripture treats that decision as rebellion because it rejects God's rightful authority.

Judges 21:25 (NSV) describes a society collapsing into chaos: everyone did what was right in his own eyes. The verse does not celebrate freedom. It warns about moral disorder. When people become their own law, the strong dominate the weak, and truth becomes flexible.

Self-rule appears in small daily forms:

- You obey when it matches your preference, and resist when it costs you.
- You treat Scripture as advice, not command.
- You keep "private sins" because you believe God should not touch that corner.
- You set your own standards and then call them "authentic."

Self-rule also appears in religion. Some people use religious activity to keep control. They serve, give, and volunteer, but they refuse surrender. They want a life that looks faithful without a heart that is submitted.

The early church fathers warned about this. They spoke of sin as disordered desire. When desire rules, God's commands feel like threats. When God rules, desire finds its proper place.

5) Track the Pattern: Desire, Justification, Action, and Covering

Sin often moves through a repeatable sequence. Naming the sequence helps you interrupt it.

1. **Desire awakens**: "I want this."
2. **Justification forms**: "I deserve this," or "This is different," or "No one will know."
3. **Action follows**: words spoken, money spent, boundaries crossed.
4. **Covering begins**: hiding, blaming, minimizing, comparing, or doubling down.

James describes this movement in a clear way: desire conceives, then gives birth to sin, and sin grows into death (James 1:14–15, NSV). James is not describing a rare event. He is describing common spiritual mechanics.

Once you see this, you can respond earlier. You can address desire and justification before action becomes a mess that harms others.

6) Recognize "Respectable" Sin Patterns

Some sins shock us. Others hide behind respectability. Scripture warns about both.

People-Pleasing

People-pleasing can look kind, but it often functions as idolatry. You crave approval, so you avoid truth. You fear conflict, so you stay silent when you should speak. Over time, your integrity weakens.

Galatians 1:10 (NSV) draws a line: if I were still trying to please man, I would not be a servant of Christ. Paul is not promoting rudeness. He is exposing divided loyalty. You cannot serve Christ while treating human approval as the final judge.

Bitterness

Bitterness often starts with real hurt. Then it becomes a settled posture. Hebrews 12:15 (NSV) warns that a root of bitterness can spring up and cause trouble, and many become defiled. Bitterness spreads. It changes how you interpret everything. It also invites revenge fantasies and cold speech.

Self-Pity

Self-pity can feel humble, but it can be pride turned inward. It says, "My pain gives me rights others do not have." Scripture calls you to bring pain to God and seek help, not to build a throne out of suffering.

These patterns matter because they often pass as "personality." Scripture calls them what they are: spiritual issues that require repentance and renewed trust.

7) Connect Sin Patterns to Relationships and Community

Sin is never only private. It affects speech, trust, and community health.

Pride damages relationships because it refuses to listen.

Idolatry damages relationships because it uses people.

Self-rule damages relationships because it rejects accountability.

That is why Scripture places so much emphasis on confession, forgiveness, and reconciliation. James 5:16 (NSV) calls believers to confess sins to one another and pray for one another. This does not mean public exposure of every struggle. It means sin thrives in secrecy, and healing often requires honest community.

Church history supports this. Many early Christian communities practiced regular confession and mutual correction, not to create shame, but to cultivate humility and protection. The point was simple: if sin hides, it grows. If sin is brought into light with repentance, it loses power.

8) Use Practical Tests to Identify Idols and Pride

You can learn a lot about your heart by asking diagnostic questions. You do not ask them to accuse yourself. You ask them to tell the truth.

- What do I fear losing most?
- What do I daydream about when I have time alone?
- What makes me angry fast?
- What do I defend without reflection?
- What do I hide?
- What do I trust when I feel unsafe?

Your answers often point to idols. They also show where pride demands control.

One question people often ask is: "How can I tell the difference between enjoying a gift and turning it into an idol?" The answer is straightforward: you can thank God for a gift and hold it loosely, but an idol demands your loyalty and punishes you with anxiety when it is threatened.

9) Replace Sin's Patterns with New Patterns

Scripture never calls you to stop sin without giving you a better path. Repentance has two sides: turning from sin and turning to God.

Here are three replacement patterns:

Replace Pride with Humility and Teachability

1 Peter 5:5–6 (NSV) calls believers to clothe themselves with humility and to humble themselves under God's mighty hand. Humility is not self-hatred. It is truthful self-placement under God.

Practice: invite correction from a mature believer. Then listen without interrupting. Write down what you heard. Pray over it. Act on one point.

Replace Idolatry with Worship and Gratitude

1 Thessalonians 1:9 (NSV) describes conversion as turning from idols to serve the living and true God. That is the core. Idols lose power when God becomes your primary love.

Practice: list three gifts you tend to treat as ultimate. Thank God for them. Then ask God to help you obey Him even if those gifts change.

Replace Self-Rule with Submission to Scripture

Psalm 119:11 (NSV) says, "I have stored up Your word in my heart, that I might not sin against You." Scripture becomes an inner guide. It confronts excuses early.

Practice: memorize a short passage that targets your common temptation, and speak it when the justification phase begins.

10) Keep the Hope Clear: Recognition Leads to Rescue

Naming sin patterns can feel heavy. Do not miss the purpose. God reveals sin so you will run to His mercy. You do not overcome pride by trying harder to be humble. You overcome pride by seeing the greatness of God and the grace of Christ. You do not escape idolatry by emptying your life of all desires. You escape idolatry by receiving a better treasure.

You do not defeat self-rule by building stricter rules. You defeat self-rule by surrendering to a wiser King.

As you move through Book 2, you will see sin's effects in conscience, relationships, and culture. But you will also see why salvation must be God's work from start to finish. For now, take a clear first step: recognize the patterns. Bring them into the light. Ask God for clean repentance and steady obedience.

CHAPTER 4

MEASURE THE HEART BY GOD'S LAW: USE THE COMMANDMENTS AS A MIRROR

Many people treat "God's law" like a relic. They picture stone tablets and ancient rules for another time. Scripture treats God's law as a gift that reveals truth, restrains harm, and guides love. The law does not save you, but it does expose what you need saving from. It also trains you to live as God's people.

In the last chapter, we named pride, idolatry, and self-rule as repeating sin patterns. Now we need a reliable measuring line. Feelings cannot measure the heart. Comparisons cannot measure the heart. God's law can. It gives clear categories for truth, worship, speech, sexuality, money, time, and relationships.

This chapter will help you use God's law the way Scripture uses it: as a mirror that shows what is in you, so you can repent with honesty and walk in obedience with clarity.

1) Understand Why God Gives Law at All

God gives law because God is King and Father. Kings set standards for life in their kingdom. Fathers instruct children for their good. God's commands are not random. They flow from His character and His design for human life.

Deuteronomy 10:12–13 (NSV) ties the purpose together: fear the Lord, walk in His ways, love Him, serve Him, and keep His commandments for your good. God's law aims at faithful living, not spiritual confusion.

So the law is not first a ladder to climb. It is light that shows the path. It is also a mirror that shows what is wrong in the heart.

2) Meet the Ten Commandments as a Summary of God's Moral Will

The Ten Commandments in Exodus 20:1–17 (NSV) give a clear summary of God's moral will. They are not the only commands in Scripture, but they function like a backbone. They teach you what love for God and neighbor looks like in concrete terms.

The commandments have a structure:

- The first commands focus on worship and loyalty to God.
- The later commands focus on life with other people.

This matches what Jesus later teaches about the greatest commandments: love God fully and love your neighbor as yourself (Matthew 22:37–40, NSV). Jesus does not replace God's moral will. He summarizes it and presses it deeper into the heart.

Are the commandments only about outward actions? No, because Scripture repeatedly shows that God aims at motives as well as behaviors.

3) Use the Law as a Mirror, Not a Mask

A mirror shows your true condition. A mask hides it. Many people use religion as a mask. They point to visible obedience while ignoring hidden sin.

Romans 3:19–20 (NSV) explains a core use of the law: the law speaks so every mouth may be stopped and the whole world held accountable to God; through the law comes knowledge of sin. That is blunt. The law removes excuses. It ends the habit of self-justification.

This is why moral people sometimes resist God's law. The law does not flatter. It names sin with precision. It exposes pride that hides behind respectability.

If you use the law as a mask, you will become defensive and harsh. If you use the law as a mirror, you will become honest and humble.

4) Learn Three Biblical Uses of God's Law

Across church history, teachers often explained the law's purpose in three broad uses. This is not a clever system. It is a practical summary of how Scripture speaks.

Use 1: The Law Reveals Sin and Drives You to Mercy

Romans 7:7 (NSV) captures it: Paul says he would not have known sin except through the law. The law exposes what hides in you. It identifies coveting, not only theft. It identifies inner desire, not only outward acts.

This use protects the gospel. If you do not see sin clearly, you will not value grace. You will think salvation is improvement, not rescue.

Use 2: The Law Restrains Evil in Society

Even unbelievers benefit from moral clarity. Laws against murder, theft, and perjury restrain harm. Social customs shaped by Scripture can reduce violence and protect families. This restraint does not change the heart. It limits damage.

The Bible assumes this function when it calls rulers to punish wrongdoing and reward good (Romans 13:3–4, NSV). The point is not that governments create righteousness. The point is that God uses order to restrain chaos.

Use 3: The Law Guides Believers in Grateful Obedience

Once you belong to God, you do not obey to earn acceptance. You obey because you are accepted in Christ, and you want to please your Father. Scripture treats obedience as the path of wisdom.

Jesus says plainly, "If you love Me, you will keep My commandments" (John 14:15, NSV). Love does not float above obedience. Love expresses itself through obedience.

This third use keeps believers from drifting into moral fog. Grace does not erase God's moral will. Grace trains you to delight in it.

5) Let the Commandments Expose Pride, Idolatry, and Self-Rule

The Ten Commandments cut through the three patterns we named earlier.

- Pride resists submission. The first command demands loyalty to God alone.
- Idolatry seeks replacements. The commandments forbid worshiping God on your own terms.
- Self-rule rejects boundaries. The commandments define right and wrong outside your feelings.

Here is a simple way to read the commandments as heart-tests:

1. **No other gods**: What do I treat as ultimate?
2. **No carved images**: Do I remake God into a version I prefer?
3. **Honor God's name**: Do I use God to decorate my plans?
4. **Remember the Sabbath**: Do I trust God enough to rest?
5. **Honor parents**: Do I honor rightful authority and responsibility?
6. **Do not murder**: Do I nurture anger and contempt?
7. **Do not commit adultery**: Do I treat people as objects?
8. **Do not steal**: Do I take what is not mine, in money or time?
9. **Do not bear false witness**: Do I shape truth to protect myself?
10. **Do not covet**: Do I resent what God has given others?

Notice how many aim at the inner life. God's law does not stop at public reputation. It reaches the heart.

6) Understand How Jesus Deepens the Law without Changing It

Some people read the Old Testament law and think Jesus lowered the standard. Jesus did the opposite. He exposed the law's true depth.

In Matthew 5:21–22 (NSV), Jesus connects murder to anger. In Matthew 5:27–28 (NSV), He connects adultery to lust. His point is not that external obedience is meaningless. His point is that external obedience can hide a corrupt heart.

This helps you see why you need more than rules. You need a changed heart. The law tells you what love requires. It cannot create love in you. Only God's grace can do that.

So the law and the gospel are not enemies. The law diagnoses. The gospel heals and renews. Then renewed people learn to obey from the heart.

7) Avoid Two Errors: Legalism and Lawlessness

When Christians talk about God's law, two errors show up quickly.

Error 1: Legalism

Legalism uses law to earn God's acceptance. It treats obedience as a payment plan. It often produces pride, fear, and hypocrisy.

Paul rejects this with force. Galatians 2:16 (NSV) teaches that a person is not justified by works of the law but through faith in Jesus Christ. Justification is God's verdict of "righteous" on the basis of Christ, not your performance.

Legalism also harms relationships. It makes you a judge who scans others for failure, while hiding your own. It turns church into a courtroom.

Error 2: Lawlessness

Lawlessness uses grace as an excuse to ignore obedience. It says, "God forgives, so it does not matter how I live." Scripture rejects that too.

James 2:8 (NSV) calls the love command the "royal law." It is royal because it belongs to the King and governs His people. Love is not lawless. Love has shape.

Both errors twist the Bible. Legalism forgets grace. Lawlessness forgets holiness. The gospel preserves both: free forgiveness and real transformation.

8) Practice Using the Law for Self-Examination without Self-Destruction

Some believers fear self-examination because it can spiral into shame. Others avoid it because it threatens comfort. Scripture calls for a healthier path: honest confession under mercy.

Psalm 139:23–24 (NSV) models this: the psalmist asks God to search him, know his heart, and lead him in the everlasting way. This is not self-hatred. It is openness to God's correction with confidence in God's care.

Use this simple process:

1. **Read one commandment slowly.**
2. **Ask what it requires and what it forbids.**
3. **Name one outward way you obey and one inward way you resist.**
4. **Confess specific sin without excuses.**
5. **Ask God for strength to change one concrete behavior this week.**

This process works because it keeps confession specific and action-oriented. It also keeps you anchored in grace. You are not confessing to earn love. You are confessing because you are loved.

9) See How the Law Protects Community Life

The commandments are not private spirituality. They protect real people.

- "Do not bear false witness" protects reputations and justice.
- "Do not steal" protects families and livelihoods.
- "Do not commit adultery" protects marriages and children.
- "Honor your father and mother" protects generational stability.
- "Do not covet" protects the heart from resentment that poisons community.

When a church treats these commands lightly, trust collapses. When believers take them seriously, community grows safer and stronger.

This is why many churches across history taught the Ten Commandments using catechisms and sermons. They wanted believers to understand sin, practice repentance, and learn the shape of love. The goal was not control. The goal was formation.

10) Keep the Main Point Clear: The Mirror Leads to the Savior and the Path

God's law is a mirror that tells the truth. It shows you God's holy standard. It shows you your real condition. It also shows you the shape of love.

But the mirror cannot wash you. It can only show the dirt. When the mirror exposes sin, you must go to the cleansing God provides. Later books will focus on salvation in depth. For now, keep one truth fixed: the law makes the need clear so grace becomes precious.

So use the commandments the right way:

- Let them humble you, not harden you.
- Let them convict you, not crush you.
- Let them guide you, not inflate you.

When you measure your heart by God's law, you stop bargaining with sin. You also begin to see obedience as the practical path of love.

CHAPTER 5

UNDERSTAND GUILT AND SHAME: TELL THE DIFFERENCE AND SEEK TRUE CLEANSING

Guilt and shame often travel together, but they are not the same. If you confuse them, you will apply the wrong remedy. You may try to silence guilt with excuses. Or you may try to heal shame with achievements. Neither works for long.

Scripture speaks to both with clear realism and real hope. It tells you what guilt is, what shame is, how they damage the heart, and how God provides cleansing that reaches deeper than appearances. This matters for discipleship, counseling, parenting, and daily growth. Many people live for years under a heavy weight because they never learned to name the problem correctly.

In this chapter, you will learn to distinguish guilt from shame, identify how each one operates, and pursue the kind of cleansing God gives through confession, forgiveness, and restored fellowship.

1) Define Guilt: A Legal and Moral Reality Before God

Guilt is objective. It describes real moral liability. When you break God's law, you stand guilty before Him, whether you feel it or not. Feelings may intensify guilt, but feelings do not create guilt.

Scripture presents guilt in courtroom terms. God is Judge. His law is good. Sin violates His law. That makes guilt more than a psychological experience. It is a moral condition.

Psalm 51:4 (NSV) captures David's clarity after grievous sin. He says he has sinned against God and done what is evil in God's sight. David does not begin by explaining himself. He begins by admitting guilt.

This is one reason the Bible treats confession as essential. Confession agrees with God about what happened. It stops bargaining. It stops pretending.

2) Define Shame: A Relational Wound and a Sense of Exposure

Shame is often relational. It says, "I am unacceptable," or "I am stained," or "If they really knew me, I would be rejected." Guilt says, "I did wrong." Shame says, "I am wrong."

Shame can follow real sin. Shame can also follow suffering that was not your fault. People who were abused often carry shame even though they did not cause the harm. Scripture's categories help you respond wisely in both cases.

The Bible shows shame as exposure and hiding. After Adam and Eve sinned, they hid. We studied that earlier. That same impulse still shapes human life. Shame pulls you into concealment. It trains you to manage impressions instead of living in truth.

A key danger appears here: shame often grows stronger in secrecy. The longer you hide, the more shame claims authority over your identity.

3) Learn How Guilt and Shame Can Work Together

Guilt and shame can overlap, but they respond to different kinds of truth.

- Guilt needs pardon and reconciliation with God.
- Shame needs covering, welcome, and restored belonging.

If you try to treat guilt like shame, you may focus on self-esteem while ignoring repentance. If you try to treat shame like guilt, you may keep apologizing without receiving comfort and restoration.

Scripture addresses both. It speaks of forgiveness, and it also speaks of cleansing and clothing. God does not merely cancel a debt. He restores a person.

4) Use Psalm 32 as a Map: Hidden Sin Makes Life Smaller

Psalm 32:3–5 (NSV) offers one of the clearest descriptions of what hidden guilt does to a person. David describes physical and emotional strain while he kept silent, then relief when he confessed.

The pattern is worth noticing:

1. Silence and concealment.
2. Inner pressure and weakness.
3. Confession without excuse.
4. Forgiveness and renewed stability.

This passage shows that guilt does not stay "spiritual." It spills into the body and into daily life. It drains energy. It tightens relationships. It produces irritability, numbness, or constant self-defense.

Confession is not a magic trick. It is the moment you step into light. It is also the moment you stop trying to be your own savior.

5) Learn God's Promise for Guilt: Confession Leads to Forgiveness

A central promise for guilt appears in 1 John 1:9 (NSV). God is faithful and just to forgive sins and cleanse from unrighteousness when we confess. Notice two words: faithful and just. Forgiveness is not God ignoring evil. Forgiveness is God acting in line with His covenant faithfulness and righteous provision.

This is where Christian theology becomes sharply different from self-help. Self-help often says, "Forgive yourself." Scripture says, "Come to God, confess honestly, and receive His forgiveness."

The difference matters. Self-forgiveness can become self-deception. God's forgiveness is grounded in God's verdict and God's mercy.

Church history has emphasized this point in pastoral care. Many historic liturgies include confession and assurance for a reason. They train believers to stop hiding and to rely on God's promise. Public worship reinforces what private conscience forgets.

6) Learn God's Remedy for Shame: Cleansing, Covering, and Welcome

God's answer to shame is not performance. It is cleansing and restored fellowship.

Hebrews 9:14 (NSV) speaks about the blood of Christ cleansing the conscience from dead works to serve the living God. This reaches into the inner life. It addresses the "stained" feeling that shame often produces.

Scripture also speaks of believers being clothed in righteousness.

Isaiah 61:10 (NSV) rejoices in being clothed with garments of salvation. Clothing language matters because shame often feels like exposure. God answers with covering that is real, not pretend.

Then Scripture adds welcome. Romans 15:7 (NSV) calls believers to welcome one another as Christ welcomed them. When Christ welcomes sinners, He does not approve sin. He brings sinners into grace, truth, and a new identity.

So shame does not get healed by trying to look acceptable. Shame gets healed as God makes you clean and restores you to belonging.

7) Distinguish True Shame from False Shame

This distinction will protect your conscience.

True shame

True shame can be an appropriate response to real sin. It can push you toward repentance. It can humble you. Yet it should not settle into identity. In Christ, your identity does not remain "unclean." God cleanses.

2 Corinthians 7:10 (NSV) helps here. It describes godly sorrow producing repentance that leads to salvation, without regret. This sorrow is not self-hatred. It is grief over sin that turns into change.

False shame

False shame attaches to things God does not condemn. It may come from abuse, manipulation, unrealistic expectations, or constant criticism. It may come from family patterns that equate worth with performance.

False shame says, "You are dirty because you exist." Scripture never speaks that way. Scripture says you bear God's image. It also says Christ restores sinners and comforts the afflicted.

If you carry shame for harm done to you, you need truth and care. You may need a pastor, a trusted counselor, and a safe community. Bringing pain into light is often necessary for healing.

8) Understand the Conscience:
Why You Can Feel Guilty When You Are Not

The conscience is a gift, but it is not perfect. It can be under-trained or mis-trained. It can accuse wrongly. It can also go quiet when it should warn.

Romans 14:22–23 (NSV) shows a conscience can be tender, even about disputable matters. That tenderness can be good, but it can also become fear-driven if you treat conscience as the highest authority.

So you must train conscience by Scripture. A trained conscience does two things well:

- It convicts you when God's Word convicts you.
- It comforts you when God's Word comforts you.

This is also why some believers struggle with recurring guilt after repentance. They confessed. God forgave. Yet the conscience keeps accusing. In such cases, you must answer the conscience with truth. Romans 8:1 (NSV) states there is no condemnation for those in Christ Jesus. That does not deny discipline or consequences. It does deny condemnation as your standing before God.

9) Practice Cleansing in Real Life: Four Steps That Match Scripture

Here is a steady, action-oriented path for dealing with guilt and shame.

Step 1: Tell the truth without editing

Name the sin or the wound plainly. Avoid vague words that protect pride. Use clear language. God already knows. Honesty is for your healing.

Step 2: Confess to God and receive His verdict

Confess with specificity. Ask forgiveness. Then receive God's promise. Use 1 John 1:9 (NSV) as your anchor, not your emotions.

Step 3: Make amends where possible

If your sin harmed someone, pursue reconciliation when it is safe and wise. Zacchaeus models this impulse by making restitution after repentance (Luke 19:8, NSV). Restitution does not earn forgiveness. It expresses it.

Step 4: Bring shame into safe light

Share with a mature believer, pastor, or counselor when shame traps you in secrecy. James teaches confession and prayer in community for healing (James 5:16, NSV). Choose someone wise, not someone who collects stories.

This is not a quick fix. It is a faithful path. Over time, truth and grace loosen shame's grip.

If you want to help others, you must speak differently to guilt than to shame.

- To guilt, you speak repentance and pardon.
- To shame, you speak cleansing and welcome.
- To both, you speak the cross and resurrection.

When someone confesses sin, do not minimize it. Do not intensify it either. Agree with God's Word. Then point them to God's forgiveness in Christ.

When someone carries shame from being sinned against, do not treat them as guilty. Do not demand quick trust. Offer safety, patience, and practical help. Remind them God sees, God judges, and God heals. Then help them take wise next steps.

Many historic pastors emphasized this kind of care. They warned against two failures: harshness that crushes the weak, and softness that refuses to confront sin. Scripture calls for truth and gentleness at the same time.

11) Keep the Center:
Jesus Gives a Clean Conscience and a New Identity

The Bible does not leave you in analysis. It brings you to Christ.

Guilt finds its answer in pardon. Shame finds its answer in cleansing and adoption. Scripture speaks of believers being made God's children (John 1:12, NSV). Children may be corrected, but they are not rejected. That relational security changes everything.

When shame says, "You are unworthy," you answer, "Christ cleanses."

When guilt says, "You are condemned," you answer, "Christ has borne my judgment."

When memory says, "This will define you," you answer, "God defines me in Christ."

You will still face consequences at times. You will still need growth. Yet you do not live under the old verdict. You live under God's grace.

CHAPTER 6

EXPLAIN HUMAN RELATIONSHIPS: STUDY MARRIAGE, FAMILY, AND NEIGHBOR - LOVE

Human relationships can be a source of great comfort and deep pain. Scripture does not treat relationships as optional. God made people to live in covenant, community, and responsibility. That is why sin shows up so quickly in the home, in friendships, and in public life. Relationships reveal what is in us.

This chapter builds a clear framework for three major arenas: **marriage**, **family**, and **neighbor-love**. You will see God's design, sin's common distortions, and practical ways to live faithfully. You will also see why the gospel matters here. Doctrine becomes visible in relationships faster than anywhere else.

1) Start with God's Design: Covenant, Not Convenience

The Bible treats relationships as covenantal, not casual. A covenant is a binding commitment that creates obligations and protection. God relates to His people by covenant, and He calls His people to live with covenant faithfulness.

Marriage is the clearest example. Genesis 2:24 (NSV) describes a man and a woman leaving and cleaving, becoming one flesh. This is not presented as a social experiment. It is a created pattern. It includes loyalty ("hold fast"), unity ("one flesh"), and a public re-ordering of priorities ("leave").

This does not mean every person must marry to be whole. Scripture honors singleness and marriage as gifts with different callings. Yet it does mean marriage, when entered, is not a temporary arrangement for personal fulfillment. It is a covenant that requires faithfulness.

2) Understand Marriage Roles as Service, Not Control

Many conflicts in marriage come from a shared mistake: both spouses try to use power rather than give service. Scripture calls for a different posture.

Ephesians 5:25 (NSV) commands husbands to love their wives as Christ loved the church and gave Himself for her. That is sacrificial leadership. It rejects harshness and selfishness. It also gives a clear model: Christ's authority expresses itself through self-giving care.

Ephesians 5 also calls wives to respect and support their husbands in a way that reflects the church's response to Christ. In faithful Christian teaching across the centuries, wise leaders have stressed that this never excuses intimidation, coercion, or harm. Scripture never gives permission for abuse. It calls for holiness, protection, and accountability.

If you want one practical summary: **husbands lead by serving; wives support by honoring; both submit to Christ and to one another's good.** When either spouse treats the other as a tool, covenant life breaks down.

3) Protect Marriage with Clear Boundaries

Marriage does not survive on romance alone. It survives on trust built through repeated faithfulness.

Malachi 2:14–16 (NSV) presents marriage as a covenant and warns against treachery. The passage treats unfaithfulness as serious because it tears apart what God intends to be a safe bond. Scripture is direct about sexual sin, but covenant betrayal can also happen through persistent deceit, financial secrecy, emotional abandonment, and cruel speech.

Here are three boundaries that protect marriage in practical ways:

- **Truthful speech:** no secret lives, no double stories, no hidden accounts.
- **Loyal priorities:** spouse and children are not competing with every other demand.
- **Shared repentance:** when sin appears, confession happens quickly, not months later.

Church history supports this emphasis. Early Christian communities taught marital faithfulness as a public witness in pagan cultures that often treated sex and divorce casually. Later pastors continued the same message, because the same temptations remain.

4) Receive Singleness as a Calling with Real Value

Some people treat singleness as a "waiting room." Scripture does not. Paul teaches that singleness can allow focused devotion to the Lord's work and undivided service (1 Corinthians 7:32–35, NSV). This does not make singleness easy. It does make singleness meaningful.

The church must treat single believers as full members, not as unfinished adults. Single believers also must resist two common traps:

- **Isolation:** withdrawing into private life instead of building strong Christian friendships.
- **Self-protection:** refusing covenant commitments in church and community because they feel risky.

A healthy church treats marriage and singleness as different paths of faithfulness, not different levels of spiritual success.

5) Build a Family Culture with Discipline and Warmth

Family is a training ground for love and responsibility. It is also a place where sin can become normal if no one confronts it.

Ephesians 6:1–4 (NSV) gives direction to children and parents. Children are called to honor and obey. Parents are warned not to provoke children to anger, but to raise them in the instruction and discipline of the Lord.

Notice the balance. Scripture does not support harsh parenting that rules by fear. It also does not support passive parenting that refuses correction. Faithful parenting joins warmth and discipline, truth and patience.

If you are raising children, aim for four steady practices:

1. **Clear expectations:** children obey better when the goal is plain.
2. **Consistent correction:** correction loses power when it is random.
3. **Quick repair:** when conflict happens, return to peace through confession and forgiveness.
4. **Daily instruction:** not only lectures, but short conversations that connect choices to God's Word.

If you are an adult child, Scripture's call to honor does not end when you leave home. Honor may look different in difficult situations, especially if parents are unsafe or manipulative. Honor can include boundaries. Honor never requires enabling sin. Yet a Christian should resist contempt, bitterness, and public shaming as normal speech.

6) Treat the Church as a Real Family

Scripture describes the church as a household, not a club. That means you belong to people you did not choose, and you learn love that is not based on similarity.

Colossians 3:12–14 (NSV) calls believers to put on compassion, kindness, humility, patience, and forgiveness, and to bind everything together with love. This is relationship language. It assumes friction will happen, and it commands a holy response.

In church history, this "one another" life formed a visible witness. Early Christians cared for widows, orphans, and the sick. Later believers built hospitals, schools, and charitable networks. These works did not replace preaching. They proved that the gospel creates a new kind of community.

The practical point is simple: if your theology is sound but your church life is full of unresolved conflict, your discipleship is incomplete. God intends the church to train believers in forgiveness, truth-telling, service, and patience.

7) Define Neighbor-Love as Action, Not Sentiment

Many people say "love your neighbor" as a slogan. Scripture treats it as a command with substance.

Leviticus 19:18 (NSV) commands love for neighbor and forbids vengeance and grudges. Love is not mainly a feeling. Love is a decision to seek another's good, with integrity and restraint.

Jesus reinforces this in Luke 10:25–37 (NSV) through the parable of the Good Samaritan. The Samaritan does not feel sympathy and move on. He acts. He crosses social hostility, offers practical help, and pays a cost. Jesus presents neighbor-love as tangible mercy.

Is neighbor-love limited to people you like? No. Jesus chose an enemy figure in that story to make the point unavoidable. Neighbor-love reaches across boundaries.

This does not mean you trust every person. Love and trust are not the same. Love seeks good. Trust is earned. You can love wisely while maintaining safety and truth.

8) Practice Forgiveness with Truth and Boundaries

Forgiveness is essential in Christian relationships, but many people misunderstand it.

Biblical forgiveness is not denial. It does not call evil good. It does not erase consequences. It does not require immediate closeness. Forgiveness means you release personal vengeance and entrust justice to God while pursuing wise steps toward peace when possible.

Ephesians 4:31–32 (NSV) calls believers to put away bitterness and malice and to forgive one another as God forgave them in Christ. The model is God's grace. Yet Scripture also calls for protection and accountability. In cases of abuse, ongoing unrepentant harm, or serious danger, love may require distance and the involvement of church leaders and lawful authorities.

Healthy forgiveness has three marks:

- **Truth:** you name what happened without minimizing it.
- **Mercy:** you refuse revenge and pray for God's work in the offender.
- **Wisdom:** you set boundaries that match the situation.

9) Watch the "Relationship Sins" That Grow Quietly

Some sins do not look scandalous, but they destroy relationships over time:

- **Gossip:** it feels social, but it is theft of reputation.
- **Partiality:** it honors the impressive and ignores the weak.
- **Harsh speech:** it claims "truth" while lacking love.
- **Refusal to reconcile:** it keeps peace at a distance but leaves wounds open.

Proverbs 18:21 (NSV) warns that death and life are in the power of the tongue. Words shape atmosphere. Words set direction. Words either build trust or collapse it.

If you want to grow in relationships, begin with speech. Then move to habits. Small changes, practiced consistently, create real stability.

10) Build a Simple Relationship Rule for Daily Life

If you want a practical rule that fits marriage, family, and neighbor-life, use this:

1. **Speak truthfully.**
2. **Act faithfully.**
3. **Repair quickly.**
4. **Serve quietly.**

Truthfully means no double stories.

Faithfully means keep your promises.

Repair quickly means do not let conflict rot in silence.

Serve quietly means do good without needing praise.

This rule does not solve every complex situation. It does shape the kind of person who can handle complex situations with greater wisdom.

Human relationships are where doctrine shows its strength. God made people for covenant life. Sin distorts that life through pride and self-rule. Christ restores it by creating a new heart and a new community. So do not treat relationships as a side topic. They are a primary field for obedience.

CHAPTER 7

ADMIT HUMAN LIMITS: ACCEPT WHY YOU CANNOT SAVE YOURSELF

Most people want a salvation story that keeps them in charge. They want a plan that says, "Try harder, be better, and God will do the rest." Scripture tells a different story. It is more honest, and it is better news. The Bible teaches that humanity's deepest problem is not a lack of effort. It is a lack of life. Sin is not only what we do. Sin is what we are apart from God's grace. That is why salvation must be rescue, not self-repair.

This chapter will show why you cannot save yourself, even with sincere religion and moral discipline. We will also show why that truth is not meant to crush you. It is meant to end false hope so you can receive true hope.

1) Start with God's Standard: "Good Enough" Is Not the Measure

Many people assume God grades on a curve. They picture God as comparing them to worse people, then giving a passing mark. Scripture never speaks that way. God's standard is His own holiness.

Romans 3:10–12 (NSV) gives a sweeping assessment of humanity: none is righteous, no one understands, no one seeks God. The point is not that people are incapable of kindness. The point is that no one meets God's righteous standard, and no one naturally seeks God as God.

This matters because self-salvation always depends on lowering the standard. If the standard becomes "better than others," then pride rises quickly. But God does not ask whether you are better than your neighbor. God asks whether you are righteous before Him.

2) Understand the Problem: Sin Reaches Motives, Not Only Actions

You can change habits and still keep the same heart. That is why Scripture exposes the inner person.

Isaiah 64:6 (NSV) shocks modern ears: even our righteous deeds are like a polluted garment. The prophet is not saying every good act is worthless. He is saying no act can stand as a clean payment before a holy God, because sin contaminates motives and aims.

Here is a common example. A person gives money, but the motive is praise. Another serves, but the motive is control. Another avoids scandal, but the motive is reputation. Outward acts may look clean. The inner life can be ruled by pride.

This is why self-salvation fails. It focuses on behavior while leaving the worship problem untouched. The heart still wants self-rule.

3) See Why Religion Alone Cannot Fix the Heart

Some people respond to guilt and shame by becoming more religious. They assume religious activity can function as a spiritual payment plan. Scripture exposes that as a dead end.

In Luke 18:9–14 (NSV), Jesus tells a story about a Pharisee and a tax collector. The Pharisee lists his religious efforts and thanks God that he is not like other people. The tax collector will not even lift his eyes. He pleads for mercy. Jesus says the tax collector went home justified, not the Pharisee.

The lesson is direct: religious activity can become pride in costume. It can hide self-trust instead of producing repentance. When religion becomes self-salvation, it produces judgment toward others and blindness toward personal sin.

This is also why churches must be careful. A church can train people to look clean while leaving them unconverted. Scripture calls for preaching that exposes self-trust and directs people to Christ.

4) Accept the Bible's Diagnosis: You Need More Than Guidance—You Need New Life

Many modern messages treat humans as basically healthy but confused. Scripture treats humans as guilty and spiritually helpless apart from God.

Titus 3:3 (NSV) describes life apart from Christ: foolish, disobedient, led astray, enslaved to passions and pleasures, living in malice and envy. That is not a flattering description, but it is honest. It explains why people return to the same bondage even after strong resolutions.

This is not meant to deny human dignity. You still bear God's image. It is meant to state human need. Image-bearers are not autonomous. We were made for God. When we cut ourselves off from God's rule, we do not become free. We become enslaved to lesser masters.

5) Learn the Key Truth: God Must Draw You, or You Will Not Come

One of the clearest statements about human inability is found in Jesus' own words.

John 6:44 (NSV) says no one can come to Christ unless the Father draws him. That is not a statement about intelligence. It is a statement about spiritual ability. Apart from God's drawing grace, people do not come to Christ with faith.

This does not remove responsibility. Scripture still calls people to repent and believe. It does mean that saving faith is not the result of human willpower. It is the result of God's merciful action that changes the heart.

This truth should produce humility. If you believe, you cannot boast as if you were wiser than others. You can only give thanks that God showed mercy.

6) Track the Church's Reflection: Why the Early Debates Still Matter

This doctrine was not invented in later centuries. It was clarified because false teachers kept returning to the same basic claim: "Humans can obey God and secure salvation by their own moral ability."

In the early church, a British monk named Pelagius argued that humans could obey God's commands without needing inward renewing grace. Augustine, a pastor and theologian in North Africa, opposed that claim. Augustine argued that sin damages the will and desires so deeply that people need God's grace not only for forgiveness, but for the ability to believe and obey.

The church addressed these debates in councils and synods. The key concern was pastoral and biblical: if humans can save themselves, then grace becomes a bonus rather than a necessity. The gospel becomes advice rather than rescue.

Later, the Council of Orange (AD 529) strongly affirmed the necessity of grace for the beginning of faith, while also rejecting fatalism. The goal was to preserve biblical balance: God's grace is necessary and effective, and humans remain responsible to respond.

During the Reformation, the same issue returned. Reformers stressed that justification is by grace through faith, apart from works, and that even faith itself is a gift of God's mercy. They were not trying to be difficult. They were trying to protect the gospel from becoming a moral achievement system.

You do not need to memorize the names to benefit from the lesson. The lesson is this: whenever the church forgets human inability, it turns Christianity into self-help with religious vocabulary. Whenever the church remembers human inability, grace becomes central again.

7) Reject False Hope: "I Can Fix Myself" Sounds Strong but Fails

Self-salvation appears in several popular forms.

Form 1: Moral Improvement as the Gospel

This approach says, "Follow Jesus' ethics, and you will be fine." Ethics matter, but ethics are not the gospel. If ethics were enough, the cross would be unnecessary.

Form 2: Identity Repair through Achievement

This approach uses success to silence shame. It says, "If I can prove myself, I will finally feel clean." Achievement can distract you, but it cannot cleanse you. It can even become an idol that deepens anxiety.

Form 3: Religious Performance to Earn Peace

This approach treats prayer, giving, and service as currency. You do them to make God owe you. When pain comes anyway, bitterness grows. The heart says, "I paid, so why did God not deliver?"

All three forms share one assumption: the main problem is outside you, and the main solution is inside you. Scripture says the opposite. The problem is inside, and the solution must come from God.

8) Receive the True Hope: God Saves the Helpless Who Call for Mercy

Admitting you cannot save yourself is not despair. It is the doorway to the gospel.

Psalm 130:3–4 (NSV) asks a question with a clear answer: if the Lord kept a record of sins, who could stand? Then it declares that with the

Lord there is forgiveness, so that He may be feared. Forgiveness does not produce casualness. It produces reverence and gratitude.

When God forgives, He does more than erase a record. He restores fellowship and begins real change. That change is not the foundation of acceptance. It is the result of acceptance.

This is where many people breathe again. They have spent years trying to prove they are worthy. Scripture frees them from that burden by saying, in effect, "You are not worthy on your own. That is why God gives mercy."

9) Apply This Doctrine in Three Practical Ways

Application 1: Stop Negotiating with God

If you think you can save yourself, you will bargain: "I will obey if You bless." Scripture calls you to surrender: "You are God, and I need mercy." Surrender is not weakness. It is honesty.

Application 2: Practice Repentance as a Lifestyle

Repentance is not a one-time apology. It is a daily turning from self-rule to God's rule. When you fail, you confess quickly. When you succeed, you give thanks quickly. This keeps pride from regrowing.

Application 3: Treat Others with Patience

When you know you are saved by grace, you become less harsh with sinners and more honest about sin. You do not excuse evil. You do not treat people as projects. You speak truth and offer help with humility, because you remember what you were apart from grace.

10) Keep the Balance Clear: Helpless Does Not Mean Hopeless

Some hear "you cannot save yourself" and assume they are stuck. Scripture does not leave you stuck. It calls you to respond to God's invitation.

The Bible's pattern is consistent: God commands what you cannot produce on your own, then God provides what He commands through grace. He calls you to repent, and He gives mercy. He calls you to believe, and He draws hearts. He calls you to obey, and He supplies strength by His Spirit.

So do not confuse inability with hopelessness. The point is not that you cannot come. The point is that you cannot come on your own terms. You come as a sinner in need of grace, trusting God's promise rather than your performance.

BOOK THREE

SALVATION: RECEIVE GOD'S RESCUE IN CHRIST

A Simple Guide to Grace, Faith, the Cross, and a New Life

CHAPTER 1

TRACE GOD'S RESCUE PLAN: FOLLOW THE COVENANTS FROM PROMISE TO FULFILLMENT

Many people treat the Bible like a stack of disconnected lessons. Scripture presents one unfolding rescue plan with a clear center: God saves sinners by grace through faith in the promised Messiah. The details develop across centuries, but the purpose stays steady. God is not reacting to history. God is accomplishing His plan within history.

This chapter will trace that plan in a structured way. We will look at promise, covenant, sacrifice, kingship, and fulfillment in Christ. We will also note how the church summarized these truths in early creeds, and how major Christian traditions have explained the Bible's unity without denying real differences in the covenants.

1) Define Salvation in Biblical Terms

Salvation includes several connected acts of God:

- **Deliverance from guilt** before a holy Judge.
- **Deliverance from slavery** to sin's rule.
- **Reconciliation with God** through forgiveness and restored fellowship.
- **A new identity** as God's people.
- **A new future** shaped by resurrection hope.

This is why Scripture uses multiple images: courtroom language, family language, liberation language, and covenant language. Salvation is not a single metaphor. It is a full rescue.

Romans 3:23–24 (NSV) states the problem and the gift: all have sinned, and sinners are justified by God's grace as a gift. That one sentence removes boasting and establishes hope.

After humanity's rebellion, God did not abandon His creation. He announced His intent to redeem. You have already seen that Scripture holds judgment and mercy together from the earliest pages. Now notice something else: the rescue plan develops through promises that God keeps, even when people fail.

God's promises are not vague. They take shape through covenants—binding commitments where God establishes a relationship, defines obligations, and gives signs that confirm His word.

A covenant is not merely a contract. A contract is an exchange between equals. A covenant in Scripture is God's gracious commitment that creates a people and binds them to Himself.

3) Track the Covenant with Abraham: Blessing for the Nations

One of the clearest covenant turning points is God's call of Abram. Genesis 12:1–3 (NSV) includes a promise that reaches beyond one family: God will bless Abram, and through him blessing will come to all families of the earth.

That promise accomplishes several things at once:

- It narrows the rescue plan to a particular line.
- It sets a global aim: the nations.
- It shows salvation is God's initiative, not Abram's achievement.

Later, God confirms the promise in covenant form. The Abrahamic covenant becomes a backbone for the Old Testament storyline. It also becomes essential for the New Testament's explanation of the gospel, because the church sees Christ as the promised offspring through whom the nations are blessed.

This is not a new invention. Paul argues this directly in Galatians 3 (you can read the whole chapter in the NSV for the flow). The point is covenant continuity: God's promise stands, and God fulfills it.

4) Understand the Exodus Pattern:
Salvation as Deliverance and Belonging

The Exodus is the Bible's great rescue event in the Old Testament. God delivers Israel from slavery and then brings them into covenant life.

Exodus 6:6–7 (NSV) captures the structure: God will deliver, redeem, take them as His people, and be their God. Notice the order. God rescues first, then calls them to obedience as His people.

This pattern matters because it shows how grace and obedience relate. Obedience does not purchase rescue. Obedience follows rescue. God saves, then God teaches His people how to live.

The Exodus also shapes how later prophets describe future salvation. They often portray coming restoration as a new deliverance, a new return, and a deeper cleansing. The New Testament then presents Jesus as the fulfillment of that deliverance pattern in a final, decisive way.

5) Read Sacrifice as Theology: Why Blood and Altars Were Central

Many modern readers struggle with sacrifices. Yet sacrifices were not random rituals. They taught Israel what sin does and what forgiveness requires. They also pointed ahead.

Hebrews 10:1 (NSV) describes the law's sacrificial system as a shadow of good things to come, not the final reality. The sacrifices taught three truths:

1. **Sin brings real guilt** and deserves judgment.
2. **Forgiveness is costly**; it is not cheap denial.
3. **God provides a substitute**, pointing toward a greater provision.

The Old Testament never suggests animals are a final solution. The sacrifices function as a God-given signpost that aims beyond itself. This prepares you to grasp why the New Testament speaks of Christ's death as the climactic sacrifice that truly cleanses.

6) Follow the Covenant with David: A King Who Will Reign Forever

God's rescue plan also includes kingship. The promise of a righteous king becomes a major theme.

2 Samuel 7:12–13 (NSV) records God's commitment to David: God will raise up an offspring and establish his kingdom. This promise is not merely political. It becomes messianic. Israel's hope for a faithful king grows, especially as later kings fail.

Psalm 110:1 (NSV) strengthens this hope by describing a Lord who reigns at God's right hand. Jesus later uses this Psalm to confront shallow views of the Messiah. The early church also used it to explain Jesus' exaltation.

So salvation is not only rescue from guilt. It is the arrival of God's rightful King who rules and restores.

7) Receive the New Covenant Promise: Forgiveness and a Changed Heart

The prophets looked forward to a covenant renewal that would reach deeper than external reform.

Jeremiah 31:31–34 (NSV) announces a new covenant marked by God's law written on the heart and by real forgiveness. This promise is not anti-law. It is anti-stony-heart. It points to inward renewal.

Ezekiel 36:26–27 (NSV) speaks in similar terms: God will give a new heart and put His Spirit within His people so they walk in His ways. This is salvation described as transformation from the inside out.

These promises prepare you for the New Testament's emphasis on regeneration, new birth, and Spirit-given renewal. Salvation is more than a legal declaration. It is also a new life that produces real obedience.

8) See Christ as the Fulfillment of the Whole Story

The New Testament does not treat Jesus as an isolated figure. It presents Him as the fulfillment of the Scriptures.

Luke 24:27 (NSV) describes the risen Jesus explaining Moses and the prophets as pointing to Him. This is a crucial interpretive key. The Bible's storyline has a center.

Galatians 4:4–5 (NSV) adds a second key: when the fullness of time came, God sent His Son to redeem those under the law so they might receive adoption. That sentence ties together promise, timing, redemption, and family belonging.

Then 1 Corinthians 15:3–4 (NSV) gives a simple early summary of the gospel: Christ died for sins according to the Scriptures, He was buried, and He was raised on the third day according to the Scriptures. This is not merely Paul's opinion. It reflects the church's early teaching and public proclamation.

9) Learn from the Creeds: The Church Summarized the Gospel Early

The early church did not create a new gospel. It summarized the apostolic gospel to guard it.

The Apostles' Creed, in its basic form, confesses Christ's incarnation, suffering under Pontius Pilate, death, burial, resurrection, ascension, and coming judgment. That creed is intentionally historical. It anchors faith in real events, not private speculation.

The Nicene Creed deepens the confession of Christ's identity, especially against teachings that reduced the Son to a creature. This matters for salvation because only a true Savior can reconcile sinners to God.

Later, the Definition of Chalcedon (AD 451) clarified that Christ is one person with two natures, fully God and fully man, without confusion or division. That protects the biblical claim that Christ can truly represent humanity and truly reveal God.

These creeds are not Scripture. Yet they show how the church read Scripture and fought to preserve the gospel's meaning.

10) Address a Common Tension: How Can One Plan Include Different Covenants?

As you study covenants, you will notice both continuity and change.

- There is continuity: one God, one moral will, one promise moving toward Christ.
- There is change: new stages, new administrations, new signs, and clearer revelation.

Christians have explained this in different ways.

Covenant theology often emphasizes one overarching covenant purpose, with different covenant administrations across history. It highlights unity and the way earlier covenants prepare for Christ.

Dispensational frameworks often emphasize distinct stages in God's dealings, with careful attention to Israel and the nations. It highlights progression and the specific features of each covenant era.

Faithful Christians hold these frameworks with varying conclusions. Yet both traditions, at their best, affirm the central truth: salvation is fulfilled in Christ, and Scripture's story moves with purpose toward Him.

Your goal as a beginner is not to pick a camp quickly. Your goal is to read Scripture carefully and keep Christ at the center.

11) Apply the Rescue Story to Your Life Now

This storyline is not only for study. It shapes daily faith.

- If God keeps covenant promises across centuries, you can trust Him in your week.
- If God rescues before He commands, you can obey without trying to earn love.
- If God provides the true sacrifice, you can stop using shame as a leash.
- If God gives a true King, you can submit with confidence rather than fear.
- If God promises a new heart, you can seek change with hope, not despair.

The rescue plan is not an abstract chart. It is the reason you can repent, believe, and keep going.

CHAPTER 2

KNOW THE PROMISED SAVIOR: CONFESS JESUS CHRIST AS GOD AND MAN

Salvation rises or falls on one question: **Who is Jesus Christ?** If Jesus is only a teacher, then the cross becomes a tragedy and forgiveness becomes wishful thinking. If Jesus is only a spiritual figure without true humanity, then He cannot stand in for sinners or bear our guilt in our place. Scripture presents Jesus as both fully God and fully man, one Person with a real human life, a real death, and a real resurrection. This is not an academic detail. It is the core of Christian hope.

This chapter will help you confess Christ as the Bible presents Him. We will look at His names and titles, His two natures, His mission, and why the church guarded these truths so carefully. Then we will apply this doctrine to worship, assurance, and daily obedience.

1) Start with Jesus' Main Title: "Christ" Means the Anointed King

"Jesus" is His personal name. "Christ" is His title. "Christ" means "Anointed One," the promised King set apart by God to rule and save.

Peter's confession in Matthew 16:16 (NSV) is a turning point: "You are the Christ, the Son of the living God." Peter is not offering a compliment. He is identifying Jesus as the long-promised Messiah, the King who fulfills God's covenant promises.

This title carries weight. It means Jesus does not merely show a path. He brings a kingdom. He does not simply advise sinners. He has authority to call, forgive, and judge.

2) Hold Together Jesus' Deity and Humanity

Scripture is clear on both truths, and it holds them together without apology.

Jesus is truly God.

John 1:1 (NSV) says, "In the beginning was the Word, and the Word was with God, and the Word was God." A few verses later, John states the Word became flesh (John 1:14, NSV). John ties Jesus to God's eternal identity and then ties Jesus to real human life.

Thomas responds to the risen Christ in worship: "My Lord and my God!" (John 20:28, NSV). Jesus does not correct him. Scripture presents this confession as right.

Jesus is truly man.

Hebrews 2:14 (NSV) says that since the children share in flesh and blood, He Himself likewise shared the same, so that through death He might break the hold of the one who has the power of death. Jesus took a real body and entered real human vulnerability. He hungered, grew tired, and wept. He did not "appear" human; He became human.

You may wonder, *why must both be true?* The answer is simple: **only God can save, and only man can represent mankind.** If Jesus lacks deity, He cannot give a saving sacrifice of infinite worth. If Jesus lacks humanity, He cannot stand in our place as our true substitute.

3) Receive the Meaning of the Incarnation: God Came Near without Changing Who He Is

The incarnation means the Son of God took on human nature and lived among us. He did not stop being God. He took on what He was not: true humanity.

Philippians 2:6–8 (NSV) describes Christ's humility. Though He existed in the form of God, He took the form of a servant and became obedient to the point of death. This is not the story of a creature rising to divinity. It is the story of the eternal Son stooping to save.

The incarnation also answers a common fear: "Can God relate to my weakness?" Hebrews 4:15 (NSV) says we have a high priest who can sympathize with our weaknesses, having been tempted as we are, yet without sin. Jesus meets human life fully, yet without moral failure. That makes Him both compassionate and clean.

4) Learn the Three Offices of Christ: Prophet, Priest, and King

Across Scripture, God's people needed three kinds of help: truth from God, cleansing before God, and righteous rule under God. Jesus fulfills all three.

Jesus as Prophet

A prophet speaks God's word with authority. Jesus does more than repeat messages. He reveals the Father. Deuteronomy 18:15 (NSV) promises a prophet like Moses whom God will raise up. The early church understood Jesus as the fulfillment of this prophetic hope because He speaks God's word as God's Son.

When Jesus teaches, He does not merely interpret. He declares: "But I say to you…" He exposes the heart. He calls for repentance. He announces the kingdom.

Jesus as Priest

A priest stands between God and people, offering sacrifice and interceding. Hebrews 7:25 (NSV) says Jesus is able to save completely those who draw near through Him, since He always lives to intercede for them. His priesthood is not temporary. It continues.

Jesus also offers the decisive sacrifice. Hebrews 9:12 (NSV) says He entered the holy place once for all, securing eternal redemption. The focus is finality. His sacrifice is not repeated because it is sufficient.

Jesus as King

A king rules and protects. Revelation 19:16 (NSV) calls Jesus "King of kings and Lord of lords." This kingship is not a political slogan. It is the final reality of history. Jesus reigns now and will bring all things into open submission at the end.

These three offices show why salvation is complete. Jesus teaches truth, cleanses guilt, and rules His people into holiness.

5) Guard One Person, Two Natures: The Church's Clear Summary

The church fought over Christology because false ideas harmed the gospel.

Some claimed Jesus was a great man adopted by God. Others claimed Jesus was a divine being who only seemed human. Both errors break salvation: the first removes true deity; the second removes true humanity.

The Definition of Chalcedon (AD 451) summarized the biblical teaching with careful language: Jesus is one Person, fully God and fully man, without confusion, change, division, or separation. The statement was meant to protect what Scripture teaches, not to replace it.

You do not need to memorize Chalcedon. You do need to keep its aim: **do not split Jesus into two persons, and do not blend His natures into a third thing.** Scripture presents one Savior, truly God and truly man.

6) See Why the Virgin Birth Matters

The virgin birth is not a decorative miracle. It serves the saving purpose.

Matthew 1:21–23 (NSV) ties Jesus' birth to His mission: He will save His people from their sins, and He will be called Immanuel, "God with us." The virgin birth signals that salvation begins with God's initiative. It also highlights the uniqueness of this Son. He is not a mere moral reformer rising from within fallen humanity. He is the holy Savior sent from God, entering humanity in a new way.

This truth does not demand that you understand biology. It calls you to trust God's testimony: God can do what humans cannot do, and He does it for salvation.

7) Receive the Meaning of Jesus' Sinless Life

Many people focus on Jesus' death but forget His obedience. Scripture includes both. Jesus lived a perfectly righteous life, fulfilling God's law in heart and action.

1 Peter 2:22 (NSV) states it plainly: "He committed no sin, and no deceit was found in his mouth." His sinlessness matters because a guilty substitute cannot bear guilt for others. A stained sacrifice cannot cleanse.

Jesus' obedience also matters because salvation includes righteousness credited to believers. Later in this Book we will explore justification more fully. For now, hold this: Jesus saves not only by removing guilt, but also by providing true righteousness.

8) Trust Jesus as the Only Mediator

People often assume they need multiple mediators: saints, rituals, personal merit, or spiritual achievements. Scripture centers salvation in Christ alone.

1 Timothy 2:5 (NSV) says there is one God and one mediator between God and men, the man Christ Jesus. The verse highlights both His unity and His humanity. He stands between God and sinners as the appointed mediator.

This does not make the church useless. It puts the church in its proper role. The church proclaims Christ, teaches His word, and shepherds believers. The church does not replace Christ.

9) Apply Christ's Person to Your Assurance

Assurance becomes unstable when you look first at yourself. Your repentance can feel weak. Your obedience can be uneven. Your emotions can swing. Scripture directs you to look first at Christ.

Because Jesus is God and man, His saving work is reliable. Because He is Priest, He intercedes for you. Because He is King, He will keep you. Because He is Prophet, He will keep teaching and correcting you through His word.

Here is one genuine question: **What do you do when you feel unworthy to come to God?** You come through Christ immediately, because your access is based on His worth, not yours. Hebrews 10:22 (NSV) calls believers to draw near with a true heart in full assurance, with hearts sprinkled clean. The cleansing is God's provision, not your achievement.

10) Respond with Worship and Obedience

Christology is never only a doctrine to recite. It is a truth to live.

If Jesus is truly King, then obedience is not optional. If Jesus is truly Priest, then confession is safe and necessary. If Jesus is truly Prophet, then Scripture must shape your beliefs and choices.

A mature Christian life grows from a clear confession: Jesus Christ is Lord. That confession will cost you at times. It will also steady you. You will stop trying to carry your own salvation. You will stop treating God as distant. You will begin to live under the care of the Savior who became man for your redemption.

In the next chapter we will focus on the cross and resurrection—how

Jesus saves by His death and victory. But never forget: the work of salvation rests on the Person of the Savior. The gospel is not a method. The gospel is Christ.

CHAPTER 3

TRUST THE CROSS AND RESURRECTION: RECEIVE ATONEMENT, VICTORY, AND PEACE WITH GOD

If you want clarity about salvation, you must look straight at two events: **the cross** and **the resurrection**. The cross answers the question, "How can God forgive guilty people without denying His justice?" The resurrection answers the question, "How do we know Jesus truly saves, and what future does He secure?"

Christ's death is not a sad ending to a good teacher. It is God's appointed sacrifice for sins. Christ's resurrection is not a comforting symbol. It is God's public declaration that Jesus is Lord, that sin's debt is paid, and that death's authority is broken.

This chapter will explain what the cross accomplished, why it had to be this way, and how the resurrection completes the gospel.

1) Begin with the Problem: Sin Creates Real Debt and Real Judgment

Many people want forgiveness without guilt, acceptance without repentance, and peace without justice. Scripture does not offer that kind of peace. It offers a better peace: peace that comes through a real payment and a real victory.

God's holiness means sin must be judged. God's love means He provides a way for sinners to be forgiven. The cross is where holiness and love meet without compromise.

2) Understand Atonement: Jesus Died "For Us"

The Bible uses several connected pictures to explain Christ's death. These are not competing ideas. They are angles on the same saving work.

Substitution: Christ in the place of sinners

Mark 10:45 (NSV) states it with sharp clarity: the Son of Man came not to be served but to serve, and to give His life as a ransom for many. "Ransom" means a price paid to secure release. The verse shows purpose, not accident.

2 Corinthians 5:21 (NSV) gives another angle: God made Him who knew no sin to be sin for us, so that in Him we might become the righteousness of God. This is the heart of substitution. Jesus stands where sinners should stand, so sinners can receive what Jesus deserves.

Sacrifice: Christ as the true offering

In the Old Testament, sacrifices taught that sin brings death and forgiveness is costly. In Christ, that pattern reaches its fulfillment. The cross is not God ignoring sin. It is God dealing with sin through a true sacrifice.

Reconciliation: Christ restores peace with God

Sin breaks fellowship with God. The cross restores that fellowship. Peace with God is not mainly a feeling; it is a changed standing. Christ removes hostility by removing the guilt that created it.

3) See the Cross as God's Plan, Not Human Chaos

Some assume Jesus' death proves history is out of control. Scripture says the opposite.

Acts 2:23–24 (NSV) says Jesus was delivered up according to God's definite plan and foreknowledge, and that God raised Him up, loosening the pangs of death. Human guilt is real in the crucifixion, but God's purpose is also real. The cross is not a surprise to God. It is the center of God's saving plan.

This matters for faith. If the cross happened by accident, your salvation rests on uncertainty. If the cross happened by God's wise purpose, your salvation rests on God's faithfulness.

4) Grasp "Justification" in One Sentence: God Declares the Sinner Righteous in Christ

Justification is a courtroom word. It means God declares a person righteous, not because that person has earned righteousness, but because Christ's righteousness is credited to them.

Romans 4:25 (NSV) summarizes the cross and resurrection together: Jesus was delivered up for our trespasses and raised for our justification. That verse teaches two truths at once:

- The cross addresses real guilt ("trespasses").
- The resurrection confirms God's saving verdict ("justification").

Justification does not mean you are never corrected. It means God's final verdict over you is settled in Christ. That verdict produces peace, not pride.

5) Receive the Cross as Victory, Not Only Payment

Some people understand the cross only as payment for sin. That is true, but Scripture also speaks of victory.

Colossians 2:13–15 (NSV) teaches that God forgave sins, canceled the record of debt that stood against us, and set it aside, nailing it to the cross. Then it adds that God disarmed rulers and authorities and put them to open shame. The cross cancels guilt and defeats hostile powers.

This does not mean Christians live without conflict. It means the decisive battle is won. Satan's accusations lose their legal force because guilt is dealt with in Christ. That is why the gospel brings real freedom to a burdened conscience.

6) Hold Together Two Necessary Truths: God's Love and God's Justice

Some people fear that justice makes God harsh. Others fear that love makes God soft. The cross shows both clearly.

Romans 5:8 (NSV) says God shows His love for us in that while we were still sinners, Christ died for us. God did not wait for you to become worthy. He acted while you were guilty.

At the same time, the cross shows that sin is serious. Forgiveness required blood, not because God is cruel, but because sin is deadly and God is holy. The cross tells you the truth about your sin and the truth about God's mercy in a single event.

7) Understand the Resurrection:
God's "Yes" to Jesus and God's "No" to Death

The resurrection is not an extra chapter. It is essential.

1 Corinthians 15:20–22 (NSV) says Christ has been raised from the dead, the firstfruits of those who have fallen asleep; as in Adam all die, so in Christ shall all be made alive. "Firstfruits" means the beginning of a harvest that guarantees the rest. Jesus' resurrection is the start of the future resurrection of His people.

This changes daily life. If Jesus is raised, then:

- The gospel is true history, not a moral story.
- Your sins are truly dealt with, not merely covered by optimism.
- Your future is not decay; it is resurrection life.

8) Apply the Cross and Resurrection to Your Conscience

Many believers struggle with repeated accusations in the mind: "You failed again," "You are dirty," "God is done with you." The cross and resurrection give you a direct answer.

When guilt accuses, you do not argue from your effort. You argue from Christ's finished work: the debt is canceled.

When shame threatens identity, you do not argue from your reputation. You argue from Christ's cleansing: you belong to Him.

When fear of death rises, you do not pretend you are strong. You stand on the resurrection: death will not have the last word.

Here is a sincere question many ask: *What if my faith feels small?* Faith is not powerful because it is intense. Faith is powerful because its object is Christ. A weak hand can still receive a strong gift.

9) Practice Three "Cross-Shaped" Habits This Week

1. **Confess quickly.** Do not let sin rot in secret. Bring it into light before God.

2. **Forgive deliberately.** Release personal vengeance, not because evil is small, but because Christ will judge justly and you are called to mercy.

3. **Serve quietly.** The cross trains you to live for others, not for applause. If Jesus served you at such cost, you can serve others with patience.

These habits do not earn salvation. They express it.

CHAPTER 4

RECEIVE GRACE THROUGH FAITH: STOP EARNING AND START TRUSTING CHRIST

Many people hear the word *salvation* and assume it works like wages: do enough good, avoid enough bad, and God will accept you. Scripture says the opposite. Salvation is a gift. It is not bought, bargained for, or deserved. God saves by grace, and we receive that grace through faith.

This chapter will clarify three essentials:

1. **Grace**: why salvation starts with God's kindness, not your merit.
2. **Faith**: what it is, what it is not, and how it receives Christ.
3. **Works**: where obedience fits after you are saved.

These truths have strengthened believers for centuries because they steady the conscience and protect the gospel from turning into a performance system.

1) Define Grace: God's Free Favor to the Undeserving

Grace is God's kindness shown to people who have no claim on it. Grace does not mean God ignores sin. Grace means God provides what sinners need through Christ.

Ephesians 2:8–9 (NSV) states it plainly: you are saved by grace through faith, and this is not from yourselves; it is the gift of God, not from works, so no one may boast. That short passage removes every ground for pride. If salvation is a gift, then boasting is excluded.

Grace also explains why Christians can have real peace instead of constant anxiety. If salvation rests on your record, peace disappears the moment you fail. If salvation rests on Christ's work and God's promise, peace becomes possible even while you grow.

A sincere question arises here: *If grace is free, will people abuse it?* Some will try. Scripture addresses that later by teaching that true grace changes the heart and produces new obedience. Grace is not permission to sin. Grace is rescue from sin.

2) Define Faith: Trusting Christ, Not Trusting Yourself

Faith is not positive thinking. Faith is not denying fear. Faith is relying on Christ as Savior and Lord.

Romans 10:9–10 (NSV) says if you confess with your mouth that Jesus is Lord and believe in your heart that God raised Him from the dead, you will be saved. The passage ties faith to Christ's lordship and resurrection. It is not vague belief in "something." It is trust in a specific Person and a specific saving victory.

Faith also includes a personal turning. John 1:12 (NSV) says those who received Christ and believed in His name were given the right to become children of God. Faith receives. It does not achieve.

Here is a helpful sentence: **faith is an empty hand that receives a full Savior.** Faith is not powerful because you feel strong. Faith is powerful because Christ is strong.

3) Distinguish Faith from "Works Faith"

Some people believe facts about Jesus but still trust themselves. They may agree that Jesus died and rose, yet rely on their morality, their church attendance, or their spiritual discipline as the real foundation. That is not saving faith. That is self-trust wearing Christian language.

Philippians 3:8–9 (NSV) shows Paul rejecting that approach. He counts his religious credentials as loss in order to gain Christ and be found in Him, not having a righteousness of his own from the law, but a righteousness through faith in Christ. Paul does not despise obedience. He despises using obedience as a way to secure acceptance.

This matters because many sincere churchgoers remain restless. They think, "I hope God accepts me," because they have not stopped trying to earn acceptance. The gospel offers a better sentence: **"God accepts me in Christ."**

4) Learn Justification's Core: God Declares, Not God Negotiates

Justification means God declares the believer righteous in Christ. God does not negotiate acceptance with you, as if salvation is a shared project where you contribute enough and God meets you halfway. Scripture presents a verdict grounded in Christ's work.

Romans 5:1 (NSV) states the result: since we have been justified by faith, we have peace with God through our Lord Jesus Christ. Peace with God is not first a mood. It is a settled relationship because the guilt problem is solved.

You may ask, *does this mean God stops caring about holiness?* No. Justification changes your standing. Then sanctification changes your life. Confusing them leads to two errors: either you try to justify yourself by improvement, or you treat improvement as optional. Scripture teaches neither.

5) Place Works in the Right Spot: Fruit, Not Root

Works matter, but they belong in the right place. Works do not cause salvation. Works confirm and display salvation.

Ephesians 2:10 (NSV) follows immediately after the grace-and-faith verses: we are God's workmanship, created in Christ Jesus for good works, which God prepared beforehand, that we should walk in them. The order is crucial:

- Saved by grace through faith (gift).
- Then created for good works (purpose).

A healthy Christian life obeys because it is loved, not in order to be loved. That shift changes everything. It produces obedience marked by gratitude rather than panic.

James also insists that genuine faith produces action. James 2:17 (NSV) says faith by itself, if it does not have works, is dead. James is not contradicting Paul. James is confronting empty claims that never produce a changed life. Paul denies that works justify. James denies that living faith remains alone.

6) Understand Repentance as Faith's Companion

Faith is not mere agreement. It includes a turning from sin and self-rule. Repentance does not earn forgiveness. Repentance is how a sinner comes honestly to Christ.

Acts 17:30 (NSV) says God commands all people everywhere to repent. Repentance means you stop defending sin, stop naming rebellion as freedom, and return to God's rightful rule.

A practical way to define repentance is simple:

- **Confession**: "God, You are right about my sin."
- **Turning**: "I will not keep walking that direction."
- **Trust**: "Christ is my only hope."

If someone claims faith yet refuses repentance as a settled posture, they are not trusting Christ. They are trying to keep Christ as a helper while keeping sin as a master.

7) Learn from Church History: Why This Chapter Has Been a Battlefield

The church has repeatedly had to guard the gospel at this exact point: Is salvation a gift received by faith, or a reward earned by performance?

Early teachers fought forms of self-salvation that treated grace as optional. Later, medieval debates often centered on how grace, sacraments, and merit relate. The Reformation sharpened the issue again, insisting that justification is by faith apart from works, because Scripture excludes boasting and locates righteousness in Christ.

Different Christian traditions have nuanced language about how faith, baptism, and ongoing obedience relate. Yet whenever the church blurs the difference between **justification** (God's verdict in Christ) and **sanctification** (God's transforming work in the believer), people lose assurance and drift into either pride or despair.

A steady rule will help you: **anything that makes your performance the basis of God's acceptance is not the gospel.** The gospel makes Christ's performance the basis.

Assurance

Assurance grows when you look to Christ and God's promise, not to your spiritual mood.

John 6:37 (NSV) records Jesus' promise: whoever comes to Me I will never cast out. That promise is not fragile. It does not say, "I will keep you unless you struggle." It says He will not reject those who come.

Growth

Grace also fuels growth. When you are secure in God's acceptance, you can repent honestly without fear of being discarded. You can face hard truths because the foundation is not your pride. It is Christ.

A sincere question appears again: *What if my obedience is inconsistent?* Your inconsistency should drive you to repentance and renewed reliance on Christ, not to self-salvation. Growth is real, and it often is slow. The believer's hope remains Christ, not personal momentum.

9) Practice Receiving the Gift in Daily Life

Here are three simple practices that fit this chapter's teaching.

1. **Preach the gospel to yourself each morning.**

   Say, "I am accepted in Christ because of grace, received by faith." Then thank God.

2. **Confess quickly, without bargaining.**

   When you sin, do not offer God a trade. Confess, turn, and rely on Christ.

3. **Obey one clear command as grateful response.**

   Choose a specific act of obedience—truthful speech, generosity, purity, or forgiveness—and do it as worship, not as payment.

Grace is not a theory. It is the ground you stand on. Faith is not a mood. It is reliance on the Savior who keeps His promise.

CHAPTER 5

BE BORN AGAIN: REPENT, BELIEVE, AND WALK IN NEW LIFE

Many people treat Christianity as behavior improvement with religious language. Scripture describes something far deeper: **new birth**. God does not merely adjust your habits. He gives you new life. That is why the Bible speaks of conversion as being made alive, being renewed, and being transferred into a new kingdom.

New birth does not mean you instantly become mature. It means you become real. You move from spiritual death to spiritual life. You gain new desires, new loyalties, and a new direction. This is also where repentance becomes practical. Repentance is not a single tearful moment. It is a turning that marks a whole life.

This chapter will clarify what it means to be born again, how repentance and faith work together, and what new life looks like in daily practice.

1) Let Jesus Define the New Birth

The clearest place to begin is Jesus' conversation with Nicodemus. Jesus does not flatter him. Nicodemus is religious, educated, and respected, yet Jesus tells him a person must be born again to see the kingdom of God.

John 3:3 (NSV) states it plainly: "Unless one is born again he cannot see the kingdom of God." Jesus is not talking about becoming more religious. He is talking about a new beginning that comes from above.

Nicodemus misunderstands, so Jesus clarifies. John 3:5–6 (NSV) explains that one must be born of water and the Spirit, and that what is born of flesh is flesh, and what is born of the Spirit is spirit. The point is not mystery for mystery's sake. The point is source. Spiritual life comes from the Spirit, not from human effort.

This changes how you think about conversion. Becoming a Christian is not mainly joining a community or adopting rules. It is receiving life from God.

2) Understand Why New Birth Is Necessary

New birth is necessary because the human problem is not only guilt. It is also bondage. People do not merely commit sins; they love sin, defend sin, and return to sin. Without inward change, the heart remains set against God.

Scripture describes this as spiritual deadness and blindness. That is why the gospel is not advice. It is good news with power. When God gives new birth, the heart begins to respond differently to truth. The conscience becomes more sensitive. Sin becomes less comfortable. Christ becomes more precious.

A common question is, "If new birth is necessary, does that mean I am passive?" No. Scripture calls you to repent and believe. Yet it also teaches that God must make you alive to do so. When a dead person rises, they truly stand, walk, and speak. Their actions are real, but the life was given to them.

3) Tie New Birth to the Word of God

God does not usually bring new birth through vague spiritual feelings. He brings it through His Word, proclaimed and received.

1 Peter 1:23 (NSV) says believers are born again, not of perishable seed but of imperishable, through the living and abiding word of God. This does not turn the Bible into a magic object. It shows that God uses truth as His instrument. The gospel message is not optional. It is the seed God plants.

That is why faithful preaching, Scripture reading, and teaching matter. People do not need religious motivation alone. They need the Word that reveals Christ and calls for repentance and faith.

4) Define Repentance: Turn from Sin and Return to God

Repentance is often misunderstood. Some treat it as feeling sorry. Others treat it as self-punishment. Scripture treats repentance as a moral and spiritual turning.

Repentance includes at least three parts:

- **Conviction**: you recognize sin as sin, not as personality or mistake.
- **Confession**: you agree with God's verdict about it.
- **Turning**: you change direction, with practical steps.

Proverbs 28:13 (NSV) captures this: whoever conceals transgressions will not prosper, but whoever confesses and forsakes them will obtain mercy. Notice the movement: confession and forsaking. Repentance does not mean you never struggle again. It means you stop protecting sin. You stop calling it harmless. You stop keeping it as a private right.

Repentance is also God-centered. It is not mainly, "I dislike the consequences." It is, "I have offended God, and I want to return to His ways."

5) Connect Repentance and Faith: Two Sides of One Response

Repentance turns from sin. Faith turns to Christ. They belong together. If you try to repent without faith, you will end in despair or pride. If you try to claim faith without repentance, you will end in self-deception.

Acts 26:20 (NSV) summarizes the apostolic pattern: people should repent and turn to God, performing deeds in keeping with repentance. Notice the order. Turning to God comes first, then deeds that fit the turn. The deeds do not purchase acceptance. They confirm that a real change has begun.

Faith, in this context, is not "I believe God exists." Faith is "I trust Christ to save me, rule me, and keep me."

6) Expect Real Change: New Life Produces New Direction

New birth does not mean instant perfection, but it does mean a new direction. A person who is born again begins to fight sin instead of feeding it. They begin to pursue obedience instead of avoiding it. They begin to love Christ's people instead of treating church as a consumer product.

Galatians 2:20 (NSV) describes the new life in personal terms: "I have been crucified with Christ. It is no longer I who live, but Christ who lives in me." Paul is not saying he lost his personality. He is saying a new center now governs his life. The old self-rule has been judged. A new life is now active.

This is where many people need honesty. If there is no new direction, no new desires, and no new conflict with sin, it is wise to ask whether the person has merely adopted religious habits without receiving new life.

7) Make Peace with the Ongoing Fight

New birth begins a fight that did not exist before. Before conversion, many people can sin with little inner resistance. After conversion, the conscience wakes up, and sin begins to feel heavier. That struggle can surprise new believers.

Do not interpret that struggle as proof you are lost. Often it is proof you are alive.

Romans 6:11–14 (NSV) gives practical instruction: consider yourself dead to sin and alive to God in Christ Jesus, and do not present your members to sin as instruments for unrighteousness. The language is realistic. It assumes temptation remains. It commands decisive choices rooted in a new identity.

The Christian life is not "never tempted again." It is "no longer ruled by sin." You may stumble, but you are not owned.

8) Learn from Church History: Why the Church Emphasized Regeneration

Across centuries, pastors and theologians stressed new birth because they saw a repeated danger: people can live inside church life without truly knowing Christ.

Augustine emphasized that grace must change the will, not merely inform the mind. During the Reformation era, many teachers stressed that justification is God's verdict, and regeneration is God's inward work. Later, revivals often returned to Jesus' words about being born again, because outward religion was common while transformed life was rare.

The point is not to chase emotional experiences. The point is to seek the reality Scripture describes: a changed heart that turns to Christ and begins a new life.

9) Practice New Life in Simple, Concrete Ways

New birth is God's work, but God calls you to respond with steady obedience. Here are five practices that fit Scripture's pattern:

1. **Speak the truth quickly.** When you sin, confess it without delay. Hiding feeds darkness.

2. **Cut access to common temptations.** Remove the "easy path" to sin—apps, relationships, websites, financial habits, or hidden routines that keep you trapped.

3. **Choose one obedience step each day.** One truthful conversation. One act of generosity. One refusal to gossip. One disciplined hour of work.

4. **Stay close to the Word.** Read Scripture daily, not to earn acceptance, but to keep your mind aligned with God's voice.

5. **Attach to the church.** New life is meant to grow in community through worship, accountability, and service.

These practices do not create new birth. They help new life grow strong.

10) Keep the Main Point Clear: God Gives Life, and You Live It Out

New birth is God's gift. Repentance is your turning. Faith is your reliance on Christ. Together, they form the start of a new life that keeps unfolding.

If you feel weak, do not wait for strength before you come to Christ. Come to Christ for strength. If you fear you have failed too often, do not hide. Confess and return. The mark of new life is not sinlessness. It is repentance and renewed trust.

CHAPTER 6

GROW IN GRACE DAILY: FOLLOW HOW GOD APPLIES SALVATION AND CHANGES YOU

Many Christians can explain the cross, yet feel unsure about daily change. They know Christ saves, but they wonder why progress is slow and why old habits still tug hard. Scripture gives a clear answer: salvation is not only something Christ accomplished in history; it is also something God **applies** to a person over time. God does not merely forgive you and leave you to figure the rest out. He calls you, joins you to Christ, gives you a new standing, brings you into His family, and then shapes you into holiness.

This chapter will explain how God applies salvation in an ordered, wise way. Christians have often called this the "order of salvation." The goal is simple: help you understand what God has done, what God is doing, and what faithful growth looks like in ordinary life.

1) Begin with God's Call: Salvation Starts with God's Voice, Not Your Search

Scripture speaks of God calling people out of darkness into light. This call is more than an invitation you might ignore. In God's mercy, it is also an effective summons that awakens faith.

2 Thessalonians 2:13–14 (NSV) says God chose believers for salvation through sanctification by the Spirit and belief in the truth, and that God called them through the gospel. Notice the link: the gospel is preached, and God calls through that message.

This protects you from pride. If you came to Christ, it was not because you were smarter than others. It was because God was kind. It also strengthens evangelism. God uses the preached gospel to call sinners into life.

2) Understand Union with Christ:
Every Benefit Flows from Being "In Him"

A believer's blessings are not scattered gifts. They are joined to one central reality: union with Christ. Scripture often describes Christians as being "in Christ," and Christ living in them.

Colossians 3:1–4 (NSV) ties identity and growth together: if you have been raised with Christ, seek the things above; your life is hidden with Christ in God; Christ is your life. The logic is direct. Your new identity shapes your new direction.

Union with Christ explains why salvation is not only a legal change. It is also a life change. You are joined to a living Savior. That union becomes the source of obedience, endurance, and hope.

3) Separate Two Works without Dividing Them:
Justification and Sanctification

Many believers either confuse justification and sanctification or split them apart. Scripture keeps them distinct while holding them together.

Justification is God's verdict. God declares you righteous in Christ. This is your standing.

Sanctification is God's transforming work in you. God makes you holy in practice. This is your growth.

Romans 8:33–34 (NSV) anchors justification with courtroom clarity: who will bring a charge against God's elect? It is God who justifies. Christ Jesus died, was raised, and intercedes. That passage settles the courtroom issue. The believer's standing does not swing daily with emotions.

Sanctification, however, is a process. It includes growth, setbacks, learning, and daily warfare against sin. A justified believer can still be immature. Yet a justified believer will not remain unchanged.

4) Receive Adoption:
God Brings You into His Family, Not Only His Courtroom

Some Christians know they are forgiven but still live like unwanted servants. Scripture gives a stronger reality: adoption.

1 John 3:1 (NSV) calls believers to see the love the Father has given, that we should be called children of God—and so we are. Adoption means you belong. You are not on probation. You are not tolerated. You are received.

Adoption does not erase discipline. Fathers correct children. Yet discipline is not rejection. Discipline confirms belonging. This changes how you repent. You confess as a child returning to a Father, not as a criminal trying to bargain with a judge.

5) Define Sanctification: God Trains You for Holiness in Real Life

Sanctification is not vague spirituality. Scripture defines it as growth in holiness through the Spirit, shaped by the Word, practiced in obedience, and expressed in love.

1 Thessalonians 4:3 (NSV) states it plainly: this is the will of God, your sanctification. God's will for your life is not hidden. It is holiness.

2 Corinthians 3:18 (NSV) describes how this happens: believers behold the Lord's glory and are transformed into the same image from one degree of glory to another, and this comes from the Lord who is the Spirit. Growth is gradual, real, and Spirit-driven.

This keeps you from despair when change is slow. Scripture expects "degrees." It also keeps you from complacency. God's will is not stagnation. It is steady transformation.

6) Expect the Fight: The Old Patterns Resist the New Life

A believer has a new identity, yet the believer still lives in a world shaped by sin, with habits formed over years. Sanctification includes conflict.

This conflict shows up in three places:

- **The mind**: old thought patterns, fears, and false beliefs.
- **The desires**: cravings that once ruled you now demand attention.
- **The habits**: routines and relationships that pull you back.

Scripture does not treat temptation as strange. It treats it as part of the Christian life. The goal is not to pretend you are beyond struggle. The goal is to learn faithful resistance with repentance when you fall.

One genuine question is common here: *If I am truly saved, why do I still feel pulled toward sin?* The answer is straightforward: salvation is real, and so is remaining corruption. God does not deny the fight; He supplies grace within it, and He teaches you to walk in new patterns.

7) Use the Means God Provides:
Word, Prayer, Church, and the Lord's Table

God does not call you to holiness and then leave you with empty hands. He gives "means of grace," ordinary channels through which He strengthens faith.

The Word

God's Word renews the mind and corrects self-deception. Regular Scripture intake trains you to recognize lies and respond with truth.

Prayer

Prayer is dependence practiced. Prayer does not earn change. Prayer receives help. It also exposes motives. People often discover what they worship by noticing what they pray about most.

The Church

Sanctification is personal, but it is not private. God uses pastors, teachers, and fellow believers to encourage, correct, and protect.

The Lord's Table

Across church history, many traditions have treated the Lord's Table as a steady reminder and seal of gospel reality. You do not come because you are worthy. You come because Christ is worthy, and because you need grace. The Table trains humility, gratitude, and unity.

The early church emphasized these practices because believers needed steady formation, not occasional inspiration. Later, the Reformers stressed the same point: God shapes His people through Word and sacrament, within a real church community.

8) Practice "Put Off / Put On" in Sanctification

Sanctification becomes practical when you replace sin, not merely resist it. Scripture teaches this replacement pattern.

A useful approach is:

1. **Put off** the old pattern (name it clearly).
2. **Renew** the mind with Scripture (replace the lie).
3. **Put on** the new practice (choose an action).

Example:

- Put off harsh speech.
- Renew the mind: God hears my words and calls for patience.
- Put on: speak fewer words, speak honest words, speak gentle words.

This is not behavior control alone. It is worship. You are learning to live under God's rule in ordinary situations.

9) Learn Assurance Wisely: Look First to Christ, Then to Fruit

Assurance is not arrogance. It is settled trust in God's promise.

Scripture gives two main supports for assurance:

- **Christ's finished work**: God justifies, Christ intercedes, and accusations cannot overturn God's verdict (Romans 8:33–34, NSV).
- **The Spirit's fruit**: real change shows that new life is present. Growth may be slow, but direction matters.

If you look only at fruit, you may panic on hard days. If you look only at claims without fruit, you may drift into self-deception. Scripture gives a balanced path: rest first in Christ, then examine your life with honesty and hope.

10) Keep the End in View: God Will Finish What He Starts

Salvation applied is not a fragile project. God completes what He begins. This is where many believers gain steadiness. Sanctification is hard, but it is not uncertain.

The same God who called you through the gospel, joined you to Christ, justified you, and adopted you is the God who will keep shaping you. That truth does not produce laziness. It produces confidence for daily obedience.

BOOK FOUR

THE SPIRIT: LIVE BY GOD'S PRESENCE AND POWER

A Simple Guide to the Holy Spirit's Person, Work, Gifts, and Guidance

CHAPTER 1

MEET THE HOLY SPIRIT AS GOD: TRUST HIS PRESENCE AND FOLLOW HIS LEADING

Some Christians speak about the Holy Spirit with uncertainty. Others speak with confidence but little biblical precision. Scripture calls for something better: reverent clarity. The Holy Spirit is not an "it." He is not a mood. He is not a mere influence. He is **God**, and He relates to God's people personally.

If you misunderstand the Spirit, you will misunderstand salvation applied, prayer, growth, guidance, assurance, and the church's unity. If you know the Spirit as Scripture presents Him, you will gain steadiness. You will stop trying to live the Christian life by human energy alone.

This chapter will establish three foundations: the Spirit's **personhood**, the Spirit's **deity**, and the Spirit's **core works** in the life of believers.

1) Start with a Clear Question: Is the Spirit a Person or a Power?

Scripture answers with repeated personal actions. The Spirit speaks. The Spirit teaches. The Spirit can be grieved. The Spirit distributes gifts as He wills. These are not traits of an impersonal force.

Jesus speaks of the Spirit as "He," not "it." In John 14:16–17 (NSV), Jesus promises "another Helper" who will be with His disciples and in them. The word "Helper" points to personal support, counsel, and presence. Jesus presents the Spirit as someone who comes alongside God's people.

Paul also speaks of the Spirit in personal terms. Ephesians 4:30 (NSV) warns believers not to grieve the Holy Spirit of God. You cannot grieve electricity. You can grieve a person. This verse also links the Spirit to God's saving mark: believers are sealed for the day of redemption.

If the Spirit is a person, then Christian life includes relationship:

dependence, listening, obedience, and comfort—not mere technique.

2) Confess the Spirit as God, Not a Lesser Being

Scripture does not present the Spirit as a created messenger. It presents Him as divine.

A direct passage appears in Acts 5:3–4 (NSV). Peter confronts Ananias for lying to the Holy Spirit, then says he has not lied to man but to God. The logic is unavoidable: lying to the Spirit is lying to God. The Spirit is not merely representing God; He is God.

The Spirit also displays divine attributes. In 1 Corinthians 2:10–11 (NSV), Paul says the Spirit searches everything, even the depths of God, and that no one comprehends God's thoughts except the Spirit of God. This is not creaturely guesswork. It is divine knowledge.

The Spirit is also included in the church's Trinitarian language of blessing and worship. 2 Corinthians 13:14 (NSV) places the Spirit alongside the Father and the Son: the grace of the Lord Jesus Christ, the love of God, and the fellowship of the Holy Spirit. Scripture does not place creatures inside this kind of sacred, covenant blessing.

So the Spirit is a person, and the Spirit is God. This matters because the Christian life is not powered by self-effort. It is powered by God's own presence.

3) Hold to the Trinity: One God, Three Persons, One Saving Work

Christians did not invent the Trinity to complicate faith. The church confessed the Trinity because Scripture revealed the Father, the Son, and the Spirit as distinct and divine, yet one God.

For the Spirit, this confession protects two truths at once:

- The Spirit is not a replacement for Christ; He glorifies Christ and applies Christ's work.
- The Spirit is not a lesser helper; He is God present with God's people.

This also protects your worship. If the Spirit is God, then His work in you deserves reverence and gratitude, not casual talk or fear-driven speculation.

4) Understand the Spirit's Core Work: He Makes Salvation Real in You

Book 3 focused on what Christ accomplished. Now we focus on how God brings that saving work into a person's life.

Scripture describes the Spirit's work in several key actions:

The Spirit gives new life

Jesus connects new birth to the Spirit's work (John 3:5–6, NSV). We have already covered that earlier, so here is the same truth from another angle: the Spirit does not merely influence; He gives life. Without the Spirit's renewing work, people remain spiritually dead.

The Spirit unites believers to Christ

Union with Christ is not a human achievement. It is Spirit-wrought reality. The Spirit joins believers to Christ so Christ's benefits become theirs: forgiveness, righteousness, adoption, and a new direction.

The Spirit assures believers of belonging

Romans 8:15–16 (NSV) taught that the Spirit bears witness that believers are God's children. We used that earlier; the point here is simple: assurance is not created by self-talk alone. The Spirit strengthens confidence in God's Fatherly love.

The Spirit empowers holiness

The Christian life is not powered by guilt. It is powered by grace applied through the Spirit. Without the Spirit, commands become crushing weight. With the Spirit, commands become a path you can actually walk.

5) Learn How the Spirit Works with the Word

Some people separate the Spirit from Scripture, as if the Spirit leads mainly through impressions. Others treat Scripture as a textbook and neglect the Spirit's living ministry. Scripture holds Word and Spirit together.

The Spirit inspired Scripture, and the Spirit uses Scripture to shape believers. When you read, hear, and submit to God's Word, you are not merely collecting information. You are placing yourself under the Spirit's instrument for renewal.

A reliable rule will protect you: the Spirit will never lead you to contradict what He has already spoken in Scripture. True guidance will align with God's revealed character and commands.

This also protects the church from chaos. When "the Spirit told me" becomes a way to bypass Scripture, correction becomes impossible and pride grows. The Spirit does not lead God's people into confusion. He leads them into truth and holiness.

6) Recognize the Spirit's Leading Without Treating It Like Fortune-Telling

Many believers want guidance about jobs, relationships, and decisions. Scripture does teach that God leads. Yet it rarely encourages you to seek secret messages. It encourages you to seek wisdom.

The Spirit's leading is often ordinary:

- He renews your mind through Scripture so you can judge wisely.
- He shapes your desires so you want what honors Christ.
- He uses counsel from mature believers to correct blind spots.
- He opens and closes doors through providence.

That means you can make decisions without superstition. You pray, search Scripture, seek counsel, and act with integrity. If you want a simple definition: the Spirit's leading is God's faithful direction that produces obedience, not anxiety.

7) Address Two Common Errors About the Spirit

Error 1: Treating the Spirit as optional

Some believers focus so heavily on doctrine that they live as if the Spirit's presence were irrelevant. The result is dry faith and self-powered effort.

Error 2: Treating the Spirit as unpredictable energy

Others chase experiences, unusual claims, and constant novelty. The result can be instability, confusion, and spiritual pride.

Scripture calls for a steady middle: honor the Spirit as God, receive His gifts with gratitude, and test everything by Scripture in the life of the church.

8) Learn from Church History:
Why the Spirit's Deity Had to Be Defended

In the fourth century, some groups treated the Spirit as a high creature. The church responded by confessing the Spirit's full deity in the Nicene tradition. The Nicene-Constantinopolitan Creed (381) speaks of the Spirit as "the Lord" and "giver of life," worshiped and glorified with the Father and the Son.

This was not political maneuvering. It was pastoral necessity. If the Spirit is not God, then God is not truly present with His people in the way Scripture promises. And if the Spirit is not God, then the Christian life becomes human moral effort rather than Spirit-powered renewal.

9) Make This Personal:
What Changes When You Know the Spirit Is God?

Three changes should follow.

You stop treating growth like self-improvement

You still work, but you work in dependence. You ask for help. You trust God to supply what He commands.

You treat sin more seriously and repentance more hopefully

The Spirit convicts, but He also comforts. He exposes sin to heal it, not to destroy you.

You value the church more deeply

The Spirit does not create isolated spiritual heroes. He forms one body. He builds unity through shared truth, shared worship, and shared mission.

10) Take One Concrete Step: Practice Daily Reliance

If you want an action step that fits this chapter, begin your day with three short prayers:

1. "Holy Spirit, help me see Christ clearly today."
2. "Holy Spirit, show me any sin I am excusing."
3. "Holy Spirit, strengthen me to obey in one specific area."

Then open Scripture and read a short passage with attention. Do not rush. Ask what it requires. Ask what it reveals about God. Then obey one clear instruction before the day ends.

Meeting the Holy Spirit as God is not mainly about having unusual experiences. It is about living with steady dependence on God's presence.

CHAPTER 2

TRACE THE SPIRIT'S WORK IN THE OLD TESTAMENT: SEE GOD'S PRESENCE BEFORE PENTECOST

Many Christians assume the Holy Spirit appears only in the New Testament. Scripture does not support that idea. The Spirit is active from the opening lines of Genesis, and His work runs through Israel's history in ways that prepare you to understand Pentecost, the church, and the Christian life.

At the same time, the Old Testament and New Testament describe the Spirit's work with different emphases. In the Old Testament, the Spirit is often shown empowering particular people for particular tasks at particular times—kingship, craftsmanship, prophecy, leadership, and deliverance. In the New Testament, following Christ's finished work, the Spirit is poured out broadly on God's people in a fuller covenant sense. If you miss the Old Testament foundation, you may either downplay the Spirit's work or speak about it without biblical structure.

This chapter will trace the Spirit's work in the Old Testament under four headings: **creation, covenant life, empowerment for service, and promise of future outpouring.** Along the way, we will note how careful Christian teaching has drawn these themes together.

1) See the Spirit at Creation: God Brings Order and Life

The first time you meet the Spirit in Scripture is not in Acts. It is in Genesis.

Genesis 1:2 (NSV) describes the Spirit of God present over the waters as God prepares to bring order, beauty, and life. This verse teaches a basic truth: the Spirit is not a late addition to God's work. He is present at the beginning, active in creation.

The Bible reinforces this later. Job 33:4 (NSV) states, "The Spirit of God has made me, and the breath of the Almighty gives me life." Scripture connects the Spirit with life-giving power. He is not a distant concept. He is the divine giver of life and order.

This matters for theology and for daily faith. If the Spirit gives life in creation, then the Spirit giving life in salvation is consistent with who He is. New birth is not strange. It is God acting according to His nature.

2) Understand "Spirit" Language: Breath, Wind, and Presence

Old Testament language often uses words that carry the sense of breath or wind. The point is not poetic fog. The point is power and presence that cannot be controlled by human hands.

Wind is real, strong, and unseen. Breath is invisible yet essential for life. These images teach reverence. The Spirit is not a tool you can manage. He is God present and active.

This also protects you from treating spiritual life as technique. If the Spirit is God's living presence, then the right posture is dependence, prayer, obedience, and humility.

3) Trace the Spirit in Israel's Covenant Life: Guidance and Instruction

The Spirit is not only about extraordinary moments. The Old Testament shows the Spirit sustaining God's people through guidance and instruction.

Nehemiah 9:20 (NSV) praises God's mercy: God gave His good Spirit to instruct His people. That is striking. The Spirit is connected with teaching and formation, not only dramatic deliverances. God shepherds His people by His Spirit.

This also explains why Scripture and Spirit belong together. God's Spirit instructs in truth. He does not lead God's people into moral confusion. He forms them through God's Word, God's commands, and God's covenant purposes.

4) Watch the Spirit Empower Leaders:
Deliverance, Justice, and Courage

One of the most visible Old Testament themes is the Spirit empowering leaders for rescue and righteous action.

In the time of the judges, Scripture repeatedly states that the Spirit came upon a deliverer to rescue Israel from oppression. Judges 3:10 (NSV) says the Spirit of the Lord came upon Othniel, and he judged Israel and went out to war, and the Lord gave victory. The pattern repeats in the book: God raises a deliverer, empowers him, and rescues His people.

Two points matter here:

1. **The Spirit empowers for service, not self-display.** The goal is deliverance and protection of God's people, not personal fame.

2. **The Spirit's empowerment does not equal moral maturity.** Some judges were courageous yet deeply flawed. This warns you against equating visible gifting with holiness. God can empower a task without endorsing a person's character.

This is a practical lesson for today. A gifted leader may still require accountability. Spiritual power does not excuse sin. The Old Testament already teaches you to separate gifting from godliness.

5) See the Spirit Equip Craftsmanship: Skill for God's House

Many people think the Spirit only empowers "spiritual" activities like preaching. The Old Testament widens your view.

Exodus 31:2–5 (NSV) describes Bezalel being filled with the Spirit of God with ability, intelligence, knowledge, and craftsmanship to build for the tabernacle. That is Spirit-given skill in design, artistry, and construction for holy worship.

This expands your theology of vocation. The Spirit's work includes wisdom and skill used for God's glory. In modern terms, God can strengthen faithful work in teaching, administration, music, care, building, and problem-solving—especially when that work serves worship and the good of God's people.

This does not mean every talent is automatically spiritual. It means God is free to supply real ability for His purposes, and believers should honor skilled work as meaningful service.

6) Trace the Spirit in Kingship: Anointing, Rule, and Responsibility

The Spirit's relationship to kingship in the Old Testament is central for understanding Jesus as the anointed Messiah.

1 Samuel 16:13 (NSV) describes Samuel anointing David, and the Spirit of the Lord rushing upon him from that day forward. The Spirit's empowerment for David connects to leadership under God's authority. Israel's king was meant to rule in obedience to God, guarding justice and honoring the covenant.

Yet the Old Testament also warns that the Spirit's empowering presence in leadership could be forfeited in a covenantal sense through hardened rebellion. This is why David prays in Psalm 51:11 (NSV), "Do not cast me away from Your presence, and do not take Your Holy Spirit from me." David is not describing ordinary Christian experience after Pentecost in the same way. He is pleading as a covenant king who knows his sin threatens the stability of his calling and the wellbeing of the people he leads.

This is a key interpretive lesson: **Old Testament Spirit language often relates to roles—king, prophet, leader—within the covenant administration.** That prepares you to see why the New Testament later stresses the Spirit's indwelling of all believers as a shared covenant blessing.

7) See the Spirit in Prophecy: God Speaks Through His Servants

The prophets did not speak as private thinkers offering religious opinions. They spoke as God's messengers.

2 Peter 1:21 (NSV) states a New Testament summary of the Old Testament prophetic pattern: men spoke from God as they were carried along by the Holy Spirit. The Spirit is tied to revelation. God's Word comes by God's Spirit.

This is why the church has always treated Scripture as Spirit-given. It also explains why prophecy in Scripture is not merely encouragement. It includes rebuke, warning, and covenant instruction. The Spirit's work is not only comfort; it is truth.

8) Grasp a Major Old Testament Tension:
Presence with Limits, Promise of More

The Old Testament shows God's real presence and real power, yet it also builds anticipation. Several passages look forward to a day when the Spirit's work would be more widespread and more inward.

Zechariah 4:6 (NSV) gives a famous principle: "Not by might, nor by power, but by My Spirit, says the Lord." This line addresses human weakness and God's sufficiency. It also points forward. God's work will not be secured by human strength. It will be secured by divine action.

The prophets also speak about a future era marked by deeper internal renewal. The Old Testament repeatedly connects hope with a change of heart and a greater work of God among His people. This prepares you for the New Testament's language about new birth, indwelling, and Spirit-given transformation across the whole church.

9) Learn from Israel's Failure: The Spirit Can Be Resisted and Grieved

The Old Testament is candid about rebellion. God's people often received mercy and still resisted God.

Isaiah 63:10 (NSV) says they rebelled and grieved His Holy Spirit. That verse is important because it holds two truths together: the Spirit is personal, and resistance is real. People can oppose God's leading. They can harden their hearts. They can reject instruction.

This prepares you to understand why the New Testament includes both comfort and warning. The Spirit strengthens believers, and believers are also commanded not to resist, quench, or ignore His work. The covenant story teaches that spiritual privilege never justifies spiritual carelessness.

10) Connect Old Testament Themes to Christ:
The Spirit Prepares the Way

The Old Testament's Spirit-work is not isolated. It is preparation for Christ.

- The Spirit gives life in creation, preparing you to see the Spirit give life in regeneration.
- The Spirit empowers leaders and kings, preparing you for the Messiah, the true anointed King.

- The Spirit speaks through prophets, preparing you for Christ, the final Word and faithful Prophet.
- The Spirit instructs and guides the people, preparing you for a fuller covenant community shaped from within.

In church history, this is one reason theologians spoke about the unity of God's saving work: the Spirit's presence is consistent, yet His covenant administration unfolds with the storyline. The Old Testament is not "Spirit-less." It is "promise-shaped." It creates categories that become clearer after Christ's death, resurrection, and ascension.

11) Apply This Chapter:
Live with Reverence, Gratitude, and Wise Expectations

Here are three practical ways this Old Testament view helps you today.

First, it keeps you from treating the Spirit as novelty.

The Spirit has been active from the beginning. You do not need constant new claims to take Him seriously.

Second, it teaches you to value character above gifting.

Judges and kings show that empowerment for a task does not guarantee holiness. Do not confuse visible ability with spiritual maturity.

Third, it teaches you to seek the Spirit's help in ordinary work.

The Spirit equipped Bezalel for craftsmanship. Pray for wisdom, skill, patience, and faithfulness in the work God has given you.

The Old Testament teaches that God's Spirit is real, personal, and powerful—present in creation, guiding covenant life, empowering service, and promising deeper renewal. In the next chapter, we will move into the life and ministry of Jesus to see how the Spirit's work is displayed in the Messiah Himself, preparing for the Spirit's outpouring on the church.

CHAPTER 3

FOLLOW THE SPIRIT IN JESUS' LIFE: SEE THE MESSIAH ANOINTED FOR HIS MISSION

If you want to understand the Holy Spirit, do not begin with debates or unusual claims. Begin with Jesus. The Spirit's work in Christ's life shows what true anointing looks like: it produces holiness, truth, compassion, and faithful obedience to the Father. It also shows that salvation is not only about what Jesus did *for* you on the cross, but also about what He did *as* the obedient Messiah—living, resisting temptation, proclaiming the kingdom, and carrying out His mission by the Spirit's power.

This chapter will trace the Spirit's role in Jesus' life from conception to ministry to sacrifice. The goal is to help you see the Spirit's work with biblical clarity and to apply it wisely to Christian life today.

1) Start at the Beginning: The Spirit's Work in the Incarnation

Jesus did not begin His existence in Bethlehem. He is the eternal Son who took on human nature. Yet the incarnation enters history through the Spirit's work.

Luke 1:35 (NSV) explains to Mary that the Holy Spirit will come upon her, and the power of the Most High will overshadow her. This is not an abstract miracle. It is God preparing a true human nature for the Son, in a holy and unique way. The Spirit's work here guards two truths: Jesus is truly human, and He is holy from the start.

This matters for salvation because a Savior who shares our humanity can represent us, and a Savior who is sinless can save us.

2) Notice the Pattern: The Spirit Marks Jesus as the Promised Messiah

In the Old Testament, kings were anointed as a sign of divine appointment. Jesus is "the Christ," the Anointed One, and the Spirit's presence marks His identity and mission.

At Jesus' baptism, the Spirit descends on Him. Luke 3:21–22 (NSV) describes the Spirit coming in bodily form like a dove, and the Father's voice declaring Jesus as His beloved Son. This event is Trinitarian, public, and decisive. It shows that Jesus' mission begins with divine confirmation.

The Spirit's descent does not mean Jesus lacked deity before baptism. Jesus is eternally the Son. Rather, it shows Jesus beginning His public ministry as the Messiah, equipped for His role as the obedient servant-king.

3) See the Spirit Lead Jesus into Testing: Holiness Before Public Power

Many people chase public power while neglecting holiness. Jesus' path is the reverse. The Spirit leads Him into testing before public ministry.

Luke 4:1–2 (NSV) says Jesus, full of the Holy Spirit, was led by the Spirit in the wilderness. This is important. Temptation is not always a sign God is absent. Sometimes it is part of God's shaping work. Jesus faces real temptation, not as a sinner, but as the righteous Messiah who must succeed where Adam and Israel failed.

He resists by Scripture. He does not argue with clever philosophy. He stands on God's Word. This teaches you that the Spirit's leading will not separate you from Scripture. The Spirit strengthens obedience, and Scripture provides the clear line.

4) Hear Jesus Describe His Ministry: The Spirit Anoints for Good News and Mercy

Jesus does not leave you guessing about the Spirit's role in His mission. He explains it openly.

Luke 4:18–19 (NSV) records Jesus reading from Isaiah: the Spirit of the Lord is upon Me because He has anointed Me to preach good news to the poor, proclaim liberty to captives, recovery of sight to the blind, and freedom to the oppressed. Then Jesus says this Scripture is fulfilled in their hearing.

This is one of the most important Spirit passages in the Gospels. It shows the Spirit's anointing leads to:

- proclamation of good news,
- mercy to the weak,

- liberation from bondage,
- visible signs that confirm the kingdom's arrival.

The focus is not spectacle. The focus is the kingdom of God advancing through truth and compassion.

5) Understand Miracles as Signs of the Kingdom, Not Performances

Jesus' miracles are not random displays of ability. They are signs that God's reign has arrived and that the curse is being reversed.

When Jesus heals, restores, and delivers, He is showing what God's kingdom does. In doing so, He also shows that spiritual power is meant for service. Jesus' miracles do not create ego. They create worship, gratitude, and amazement at God's mercy.

This corrects a modern temptation: to treat spiritual power as status. In Christ, power serves love. Any claim of Spirit-power that produces pride, manipulation, or harm is already out of step with Jesus.

6) See the Spirit and the Father's Will Working Together

In Jesus' life, the Spirit's power never competes with the Father's will. The Spirit leads Jesus into obedience, suffering, and faithful endurance.

Jesus' ministry includes joy and compassion, but it also includes conflict, rejection, and ultimately the cross. The Spirit's presence does not guarantee an easy path. It guarantees faithful obedience and divine strength to complete the mission.

This matters for believers. If you assume the Spirit's presence means life will be simple, you will become confused when hardship comes. Jesus' Spirit-filled life included suffering with purpose.

7) Understand Christ's Obedience as Representative: He Succeeds Where We Failed

Jesus lived in full obedience not only as an example, but also as the representative Messiah. He stands in the place of His people. His obedience fulfills righteousness.

This connects the Spirit's work to salvation directly. The Spirit empowered Jesus' human life for obedient service. Then Jesus offers His obedient life and atoning death as the ground of salvation.

This is not a small detail. If Jesus is only an example, you are left trying to imitate Him without hope. If Jesus is Savior and representative, you can imitate Him from a secure position, not to earn acceptance.

8) Learn What True Anointing Produces: Fruit Before Gifts

If you want a simple test of Spirit-work, look at Jesus:

- humility instead of self-promotion,
- truth instead of manipulation,
- compassion instead of contempt,
- purity instead of compromise,
- endurance instead of quitting.

This does not mean gifts are unimportant. It means fruit is the first evidence of the Spirit's work. Gifts can be counterfeited or misused. Christlike character cannot be faked for long.

A church that seeks gifts without seeking Christlike character will eventually drift into confusion. A believer who seeks experiences without seeking holiness will eventually be disappointed.

9) Connect Jesus' Ministry to the Promise of the Spirit for Believers

Jesus' Spirit-anointed life is not meant to remain unique and distant. It prepares for the Spirit's outpouring on the church.

Jesus promises that His followers will receive the Spirit in a new covenant fullness after His work is finished. The Gospels present Jesus as the one who baptizes with the Holy Spirit, bringing God's presence to His people in a deeper way.

So the Spirit's work in Jesus is both model and foundation: it shows what Spirit-empowered faithfulness looks like, and it prepares the way for believers to live by the Spirit as those united to Christ.

10) Apply This Chapter: Follow Christ's Pattern in Three Ways

First, pursue holiness before influence.

The Spirit led Jesus into the wilderness before the crowds. Do not rush past hidden obedience.

Second, tie guidance to Scripture.

Jesus resisted temptation with God's Word. Do not treat impressions as higher than Scripture.

Third, serve with compassion.

Jesus' Spirit-anointed ministry brought good news to the poor and help to the afflicted. Measure your "spiritual life" by whether it produces patient love.

When you study the Spirit in Jesus' life, you gain a stable picture of true Spirit-work. It is not chaotic. It is not self-centered. It is Christ-centered and Father-pleasing. In the next chapter, we will move from Jesus' ministry to the Spirit's arrival in the early church, especially at Pentecost, and we will see what changed and what remained consistent with the Old Testament foundation.

CHAPTER 4

RECEIVE THE SPIRIT'S PROMISE: UNDERSTAND PENTECOST AND THE CHURCH'S NEW COVENANT STRENGTH

Pentecost can sound like a single striking day with unusual sounds and foreign languages. Scripture presents it as far more than a memorable moment. Pentecost is the public launch of the new covenant era, when the risen Jesus pours out the Holy Spirit on His people. It confirms that Jesus reigns, that the gospel will go to the nations, and that ordinary believers will be equipped for witness, holiness, prayer, and unity.

This chapter will explain what happened at Pentecost, why it mattered, how it connects to Old Testament promises, and how the Spirit's work spread from Jerusalem outward.

1) Place Pentecost in the Story: From Feast to Fulfillment

Pentecost was already a major Jewish feast, celebrated fifty days after Passover. Israel gathered to give thanks for God's provision. In God's timing, that feast became the stage for a greater gift: not grain, but God's own Spirit given to God's people. The timing matters. The cross occurred at Passover, the resurrection followed, and the Spirit's outpouring came at Pentecost. God was teaching the church to read redemption as a connected whole.

2) Observe the Event: The Spirit Comes with Clear Signs

Acts 2:1-4 (NSV) describes the disciples gathered together when a sound like a mighty wind filled the house, tongues as of fire appeared, and they were filled with the Holy Spirit and began to speak in other tongues as the Spirit gave them utterance. These signs were not entertainment. They were signals. Wind and fire echo God's presence in

Scripture, and the tongues served a mission purpose: the gospel would cross language barriers.

It is also important to notice what the passage emphasizes: the Spirit fills, the people speak, and God is making a public statement. Pentecost is not mainly about private spirituality. It is about God equipping public testimony to Christ.

3) Connect Pentecost to Prophecy: God Keeps His Word

Peter explains the event by appealing to prophecy. He cites Joel to show that God had promised an outpouring of the Spirit on "all flesh," including sons and daughters, young and old, servants and handmaids. Acts 2:16–18 (NSV) presents this as fulfillment, not novelty. The point is breadth: the Spirit will not be limited to a small group of leaders. In the new covenant era, God gives His Spirit broadly to His people.

This does not erase roles in the church. Pastors, teachers, and elders still matter. Yet Pentecost signals that every believer is personally involved in the life of the Spirit, the confession of Christ, and the mission of witness.

4) Hear the Main Message: The Spirit Exalts the Risen Jesus

Pentecost is not a Spirit-centered celebration that forgets Christ. Peter's sermon centers on Jesus' death, resurrection, and exaltation. The Spirit's arrival is presented as evidence that Jesus is enthroned and active.

John 16:14 (NSV) captures the same principle from Jesus' teaching: the Spirit will glorify Christ. If the Spirit's work in a church or in a life does not draw attention to Christ's lordship, Christ's gospel, and Christ's commands, something is out of alignment. The Spirit does not compete with Jesus. He makes Jesus known and trusted.

5) Track the Immediate Fruit: Conviction, Repentance, and a New Community

Acts 2 records that the crowd is cut to the heart and asks what to do. Peter calls them to repent, and the passage describes many being added to the church. Then the text highlights ordinary church life: teaching, fellowship, breaking bread, and prayers (Acts 2:42, NSV). The Spirit's strength shows itself in a new community with new priorities.

This guards you from a common error: treating the Spirit's work as only the spectacular. Pentecost includes signs, but it produces steady practices. A Spirit-filled church is never merely loud; it is devoted, generous, prayerful, and anchored in apostolic teaching.

6) Understand Languages as Mission: God Opens the Nations

The tongues at Pentecost were understood languages, heard by people from many regions. The message was not secret. It was public and intelligible. God was reversing Babel's scattering for gospel purposes, not by erasing languages, but by enabling the message to cross them.

This matters for the church's calling. The Spirit is the engine of global mission. He pushes the church outward, beyond comfort, beyond cultural walls, and beyond fear. A church that claims to be Spirit-led yet avoids witness and mercy is resisting the Spirit's purpose.

7) Follow the Expansion: From Jerusalem to the Ends of the Earth

Acts continues the Pentecost pattern as the gospel spreads. When the believers pray under pressure, the Spirit strengthens them for bold speech. Acts 4:31 (NSV) says they were filled with the Holy Spirit and continued to speak the word of God with boldness. Again, the emphasis is witness, not self-display.

Later, the Spirit's gift reaches Gentiles in a decisive way. Acts 10:44–48 (NSV) describes the Holy Spirit falling on those who heard the word, leading the Jewish believers to recognize that God grants the same gift to the nations. This moment shows Pentecost's reach. The Spirit unites Jews and Gentiles in one gospel.

8) Learn from Early Church Teaching: Guard Unity, Test Claims

Because the Spirit is active, the church had to learn discernment. The apostles insisted that the Spirit's work be tested by the apostolic gospel and by the confession of Jesus as Lord. As the church grew, it also had to reject teachings that reduced the Spirit to a creature or treated Him as an impersonal energy.

In the fourth century, the church clarified in its creedal language that the Spirit is "Lord" and "giver of life," worthy of worship with the Father and the Son. This was not an attempt to add to Scripture. It was an attempt to protect what Scripture already taught, so churches would pray, worship, and live with correct reverence.

9) Apply Pentecost Today: Seek the Spirit's Aims, Not Mere Sensations

Pentecost teaches you what to pray for. Ask for courage to witness, strength to obey, and love that builds the church. Ask for conviction that leads to repentance, and comfort that leads to endurance. Ask for unity that crosses social and cultural lines.

Also learn this: the Spirit often works through ordinary means. He uses Scripture preached and read. He uses prayer in the gathered church. He uses repentance practiced quickly. He uses faithful service that gets little notice. If you measure the Spirit's work only by what feels unusual, you will miss much of what He is doing.

10) Keep the Center: The Spirit Brings Christ's Presence to Christ's People

Pentecost does not replace Jesus. It makes Jesus' saving reign personally present to His people. The Spirit unites believers to Christ, equips witness to Christ, and forms a community that obeys Christ. When you keep that center, Pentecost becomes steady ground, not confusion.

In the next chapter, we will study the Spirit's indwelling and filling in daily Christian life, including how to pursue holiness without fear and how to discern true guidance with clarity.

CHAPTER 5

LIVE FILLED WITH THE SPIRIT: PRACTICE DAILY DEPENDENCE, HOLINESS, AND WISDOM

After Pentecost, many believers ask a practical question: what does it mean to live "filled with the Spirit" on an ordinary Tuesday? Scripture does not present Spirit-filled life as rare or unpredictable. It presents it as steady dependence on God, expressed through prayer, obedience, love, and courage. The Spirit's presence is God's gift to every believer, and Scripture also commands believers to be filled and to walk by the Spirit. That means God supplies real help, and believers respond with real choices each day.

This chapter explains the difference between the Spirit's indwelling and the Spirit's filling, how to pursue holiness without fear, and how to seek guidance without superstition. The aim is a stable practical Christian life that honors Christ in speech, desires, decisions, and relationships.

1) Distinguish Indwelling and Filling

The Spirit's indwelling is God's abiding presence in the believer. Filling is the Spirit's active influence and strengthening that shapes behavior and witness in a given moment.

Paul's command in Ephesians 5:18 (NSV) is direct: do not get drunk with wine, but be filled with the Spirit. Drunkenness is an image of control. Wine controls the mind and actions. Paul contrasts that with the Spirit's control, which leads to worship, gratitude, and love. The command is given to the church, which implies this is normal Christian life, not a special tier.

Indwelling is not lost every time you sin. Believers may grieve the Spirit, but God does not treat His children as temporary guests. Filling, however, can be resisted. You can live in ways that dull the conscience and weaken prayer. That is why Scripture calls you to seek the Spirit's

148

filling as an ongoing pattern.

2) Look for the First Evidence: Christlike Character

The Spirit's work is seen first in character, not in visibility. Galatians 5:22–23 (NSV) lists the fruit of the Spirit: love, joy, peace, patience, kindness, goodness, faithfulness, gentleness, and self-control. Fruit grows over time. It shows a living root. It also gives you a simple test: is my life becoming more like Christ?

These traits are not personality types. They are moral qualities produced as the Spirit shapes the heart. A believer may have gifts and still lack gentleness. Scripture does not treat that as a minor issue. The Spirit forms Christlike people.

3) Learn the Battle Plan: Walk by the Spirit

Galatians 5:16 (NSV) gives a daily instruction: walk by the Spirit, and you will not gratify the desires of the flesh. "Flesh" means the old patterns of self-rule. Walking is steady. It is step after step. That is the right image for sanctification.

Walking by the Spirit includes decisions. You do not drift into holiness. You choose it with help. A useful pattern is: name the temptation, reject the lie behind it, and replace it with obedience. If the temptation is anger, reject the lie that you must defend your pride, and replace it with patient speech. If the temptation is lust, reject the lie that pleasure is your right, and replace it with guarded eyes and honest confession.

4) Use the Means God Gives: Word, Prayer, and the Church

The Spirit can act in any way He chooses. Yet Scripture shows He commonly works through ordinary means.

First, the Word. The Spirit inspired Scripture, and He uses it to correct and renew the mind. If you starve Scripture, you will be driven by impulse. If you feed on Scripture, your mind gains clarity.

Second, prayer. Prayer is dependence in action. Ask for wisdom before decisions. Ask for strength in temptation. Ask for love when you feel cold. The Spirit helps believers pray in weakness, shaping requests that fit God's will.

Third, the church. The Spirit unites believers into one body, and He uses other Christians to encourage, correct, and support. Isolation makes temptation louder and shame stronger. A faithful church life gives protection and perspective.

5) Seek Guidance Wisely: Replace Superstition with Wisdom

Believers often want guidance in big choices: marriage, work, moving, conflict, and money. Scripture does teach God leads His people. Yet it rarely tells you to hunt for secret signs. It calls you to pursue wisdom.

James 1:5 (NSV) says if any of you lacks wisdom, let him ask God, who gives generously. Wisdom is the skill of living faithfully. The Spirit's guidance often looks like a renewed mind, sober evaluation of options, godly counsel, and a conscience shaped by Scripture.

Ask three grounding questions:

1. Does this choice align with God's commands?
2. Does it reflect love for neighbor and integrity?
3. Is my motive clean, or am I protecting an idol?

When you cannot see a single "perfect" option, choose the wisest option you can, then act in faith and humility. God can redirect you. His leading is not fragile.

6) Address Spiritual Dryness: What to Do When You Feel Nothing

Many believers assume the Spirit's work must always be felt. Scripture teaches that faith rests on God's promise, not on constant emotional warmth. Dryness can come from fatigue, stress, unconfessed sin, neglected prayer, or seasons of testing.

Return to basic obedience. Confess what you know is wrong. Read Scripture even when you feel dull. Pray short, honest prayers. Serve someone quietly. Meet with believers. Over time, the Spirit often restores joy through ordinary faithfulness.

Psalm 143:10 (NSV) models a wise request: teach me to do Your will, for You are my God; let Your good Spirit lead me on level ground. The prayer is not about excitement. It is about obedience.

7) Avoid Two Ditches: Quenching and Controlling

Scripture warns against quenching the Spirit, which includes resisting conviction, despising true teaching, and clinging to sin. A quenched life often looks busy but cold, informed but proud, religious but unchanged.

Scripture also warns against trying to control the Spirit, as if God exists to validate our plans. This posture appears when someone uses "God told me" to end a conversation and avoid correction. The Spirit does not make you unaccountable. He makes you teachable.

8) Practice Filling in Daily Life: Five Habits

1. Begin the day with surrender: "Lord, rule my thoughts and words today."
2. Read a short passage of Scripture and obey one clear instruction from it.
3. Confess quickly when you sin; do not rehearse excuses.
4. Choose one act of love that costs you time, comfort, or pride.
5. End the day with gratitude, naming three specific mercies.

These habits do not earn the Spirit's presence. They place you where His work is welcomed rather than resisted.

9) Keep the Main Point Clear

The Spirit's filling is not mainly about unusual experiences. It is about daily Christlike life. He forms a believer who speaks truthfully, loves steadily, repents quickly, and serves faithfully. As you pursue that aim, you will grow in stability and usefulness in the church's mission, because the Spirit's strength produces humble courage.

In the next chapter, we will examine spiritual gifts and their purpose in the church, including how to value gifts without making them the measure of maturity.

CHAPTER 6

ENDURE WITH THE SPIRIT'S COMFORT: FACE SUFFERING, STAND FIRM, AND KEEP HOPE

Sooner or later every believer discovers a hard truth: knowing sound doctrine does not remove pain. Illness still comes. Betrayal still cuts. Work can fail. Loved ones die. Fear can rise in the night even when the mind knows the gospel. In those moments, Christians need more than information. They need God's presence. Scripture teaches that God provides that presence through the Holy Spirit, who comforts, strengthens, and steadies believers for endurance.

This chapter explains how the Spirit supports Christians in suffering. We will address why suffering does not mean abandonment, how the Spirit helps in weakness, how to pray when words fail, and how hope grows in the middle of grief. The aim is not to give neat answers. The aim is to help you stand with faith when life is heavy.

1) Reject a Common Lie: Suffering Does Not Prove God Is Absent

Many believers assume that if they were truly walking with God, life would become easier. Scripture corrects that assumption. Jesus warned His disciples that trouble would come and that persecution would come. The Spirit's presence is not a guarantee of comfort. It is a guarantee of help.

John 14:26–27 (NSV) includes Jesus' promise that the Helper will teach and remind, and Jesus gives peace that is not like the world's peace. This peace is not the absence of problems. It is a settled confidence in the Father's care, even when circumstances remain painful.

This matters because suffering often tempts you to interpret God's love by your circumstances. Scripture calls you to interpret your circumstances by God's love revealed in Christ.

2) Receive the Spirit as Helper: God Comes Near to the Weak

Jesus calls the Spirit "Helper." That is not weak language. It means God gives active support to believers who cannot carry life by themselves.

Suffering exposes limits. It forces you to admit you cannot control outcomes. The Spirit meets you there. He does not merely observe. He helps.

The Spirit's help often looks ordinary: strength to get out of bed, clarity to speak one truthful sentence, patience to endure a long hospital wait, restraint when anger rises, courage to ask for prayer, humility to receive help. These may look small to outsiders, but they are often evidence of real grace.

3) Learn How the Spirit Helps You Pray When You Are Worn Down

In suffering, prayer can feel impossible. Words can dry up. The mind can race. Shame can silence you. Scripture addresses that reality with direct comfort.

Romans 8:26–27 (NSV) says the Spirit helps our weakness. We do not know what to pray for as we ought, but the Spirit Himself intercedes for us with groanings too deep for words. The passage does not romanticize pain. It speaks of groaning. Yet it anchors hope: the Spirit intercedes according to God's will.

This means your prayer life does not collapse when your emotions collapse. Even when you cannot form polished sentences, you can still come. A short prayer like "Lord, help" can be sincere faith. The Spirit is not waiting for eloquence. He helps weakness.

4) Hold on to Adoption: The Spirit Teaches You to Cry "Father"

Suffering can make you feel like an outsider. It can make you think, "God must be punishing me," or "God must love others more." Scripture counters that with adoption.

Romans 8:15 (NSV) says believers received the Spirit of adoption by whom we cry, "Abba, Father." That word "cry" matters. It suggests urgency and emotion. In suffering, the Spirit presses you toward God rather than away from God. He trains you to pray like a child, not like a worker begging for wages.

This does not remove discipline when believers sin. Yet discipline is not rejection. A Father corrects children because they belong. In suffering, do not assume God's nearness is measured by comfort. God's nearness is measured by covenant promise, and the Spirit confirms that promise in the believer's heart.

5) Understand Weakness as a Place Where God Shows Strength

Many Christians only accept weakness in theory. In practice, they treat weakness as failure. Scripture treats weakness as an arena where God's strength becomes visible.

The Spirit's comfort does not always remove the thorn. Often it supplies endurance. The Spirit teaches believers to rely on God's strength rather than their own. This reliance is not passive resignation. It is active trust: "I cannot carry this, but God will."

This is why some believers grow in humility and kindness through suffering. Suffering strips away self-sufficiency. The Spirit replaces it with dependence that is steady and realistic.

6) Receive Hope as a Present Anchor, Not a Future Escape

Christian hope is not fantasy. It is rooted in God's promises, Christ's resurrection, and the Spirit's pledge.

Ephesians 1:13–14 (NSV) says believers were sealed with the promised Holy Spirit, who is the guarantee of our inheritance until we acquire possession of it. The Spirit is not only comfort for the moment. He is God's pledge that the future is real.

This matters because suffering often narrows your vision to the next hour. The Spirit widens your vision to the full story: God will finish what He began. The believer's future is not endless loss. It is resurrection life with God.

Hope does not deny grief. Hope gives grief a boundary. Grief is real, but it is not ultimate.

7) Learn How the Spirit Builds Endurance Through the Church

The Spirit rarely comforts in isolation. He comforts through the body of Christ. Many believers try to suffer alone, thinking that asking for help is weakness. Scripture treats shared burdens as normal Christian life.

When believers pray for one another, speak Scripture to one another, and show practical care, the Spirit is at work. Comfort is often delivered through meals, visits, truthful words, and steady presence. This is why detachment from the church is so dangerous in suffering. Isolation makes fear louder and hope quieter.

A practical step is simple: name your need to mature believers and ask for prayer. Not as a performance. As a child asking family for help.

8) Guard Your Mind: The Spirit Uses Truth to Resist Despair

Suffering can magnify lies: "Nothing will change," "God does not care," "I am alone," "This proves I am cursed." The Spirit combats these lies with truth. He reminds believers of Christ, of God's promises, and of the church's hope.

This does not always feel dramatic. Often it is slow: returning to Scripture, repeating promises, rejecting hopeless self-talk, choosing worship when you do not feel like worshiping. These choices are not hypocrisy. They are faith.

This is also why the Spirit's comfort should never be separated from Scripture. Comfort without truth becomes empty reassurance. Truth without comfort becomes cold. The Spirit provides both.

9) Practice Lament: Honest Prayer Without Accusation

Scripture includes lament because believers need words for sorrow. Lament is not rebellion. It is faithful honesty that brings pain to God rather than turning pain into unbelief.

Lament includes three movements:

1. Tell God what hurts.
2. Ask God for help.
3. Reaffirm trust in God's character.

The Spirit helps believers lament. He does not demand fake cheerfulness. He leads believers to bring grief into God's presence with reverence and hope.

A short lament can be as simple as: "Father, this hurts. I am afraid. Help me trust You and do what is right today." That is not sophisticated. It is faithful.

10) Endure with a Clear Focus:
The Spirit Shapes You for Witness in Pain

Suffering often places you in front of people who are watching. They may not listen to sermons, but they will watch how you carry grief. The Spirit can use your endurance as witness, not because you are impressive, but because Christ is sustaining you.

This does not mean you must always look strong. A humble confession—"I am struggling, but God is helping me"—often carries more weight than polished speech.

The Spirit comforts so believers endure. The Spirit strengthens so believers obey. The Spirit gives hope so believers do not quit.

CHAPTER 7

GUARD UNITY BY THE SPIRIT: BUILD PEACE, PRACTICE TRUTH, AND KEEP THE CHURCH STRONG

A church can confess right doctrine and still fracture. Personal offense, rivalry, fear, and careless speech can pull believers apart faster than a false teacher. Scripture treats unity as a spiritual matter, not a social preference. Unity is the Spirit's work, and it is also the believer's responsibility. The Spirit creates one people in Christ, and believers are commanded to protect that unity through humility, patience, and truth.

This chapter shows how the Spirit produces unity, what threatens unity, and what ordinary practices keep a church steady. The goal is not shallow agreement. The goal is peace rooted in the gospel, where believers can disagree on lesser matters without breaking fellowship, and where sin is confronted without cruelty.

1) Begin with Jesus' Prayer: Unity Is a Gospel Witness

Before the cross, Jesus prayed for His people. John 17:21 (NSV) records Jesus asking that believers may all be one, so that the world may believe that the Father sent the Son. Unity is connected to the credibility of the church's witness. When believers live in constant hostility, they announce a different message than the one they preach.

This does not mean unity requires pretending. It means unity requires shared center. The center is Christ: His gospel, His lordship, His commands, and His love.

2) Confess One Body: Unity Is Created, Not Manufactured

Unity is not built by clever programs. Unity is a spiritual reality created by God when He joins believers to Christ.

Romans 12:5 (NSV) says that though many, we are one body in Christ, and individually members of one another. The church is not a crowd of customers. It is a body with shared life. This changes how you treat other believers. You treat them as family you are responsible to love.

Psalm 133:1 (NSV) celebrates this: how good and pleasant it is when brothers dwell in unity. The Psalm does not claim unity is effortless. It claims unity is worth protecting because it reflects God's own goodness.

3) Learn the Spirit's Method: Unity Grows Through Humility

Pride is the quickest path to division. Pride turns every disagreement into a threat, every correction into an insult, and every preference into a demand. The Spirit produces humility, which makes unity possible.

1 Peter 3:8 (NSV) calls believers to be harmonious, sympathetic, brotherly, tenderhearted, and humble-minded. These are not optional virtues for "nice" Christians. They are survival skills for church life.

Humility does not mean weakness. It means you can say, "I might be wrong," and "Your good matters to me," and "I will not treat my preference as a law."

4) Name the Main Threats: What Breaks Unity in Real Churches

Most church divisions do not begin with major doctrine. They begin with ordinary sins that are tolerated.

- Gossip: it spreads suspicion while hiding behind "concern."
- Rivalry: it treats ministry as competition.
- Partiality: it honors the impressive and ignores the quiet.
- Unresolved offense: it turns pain into distance instead of conversation.
- Harsh certainty: it speaks truth without love and calls it courage.

The Spirit does not bless these patterns. They grieve the church and weaken witness. If a church wants unity, it must treat these sins as serious.

5) Practice Truth-Telling: Unity Without Truth Is Fragile

Some churches fear conflict so much that they avoid truth. That kind of unity is thin. It breaks under pressure.

1 Corinthians 1:10 (NSV) urges believers to agree and that there be no divisions, but that they be united in the same mind and judgment. Paul writes this to a church filled with party spirit. His solution is not silence. His solution is shared commitment to Christ and to clear teaching.

Truth-telling includes doctrinal clarity, but it also includes honest conversation. It means you do not weaponize silence. You speak, but you speak for the good of the other.

6) Handle Conflict with a Spirit-Guided Process

Conflict is unavoidable where sinners gather. The difference between a healthy church and an unhealthy church is not the presence of conflict, but the way conflict is handled.

A Spirit-guided process is simple and demanding:

1. Go directly. Do not recruit allies first.
2. Speak specifically. Vague accusations multiply resentment.
3. Listen carefully. You may have misunderstood.
4. Confess what is yours. Repentance disarms pride.
5. Seek a clear next step.

Galatians 6:1–2 (NSV) gives the church a tone for restoration: if someone is caught in a trespass, those who are spiritual should restore him in a spirit of gentleness, watching themselves, and bearing one another's burdens. Restoration requires truth. Gentleness requires humility.

7) Make Room for Differences: Wisdom on "Disputable Matters"

Unity does not require uniformity. Churches include different backgrounds, cultures, and temperaments. Wise Christians learn to distinguish between core gospel truths and secondary questions.

Core truths are non-negotiable: the person of Christ, the gospel of grace, the authority of Scripture, the call to holiness. Secondary matters include many preferences and some theological questions that faithful believers have debated without breaking the faith.

The Spirit helps believers hold convictions without contempt. He trains you to say, "I have a view, and I can still honor you," and "I can disagree without questioning your faith."

One practical safeguard is shared confession. When a church regularly admits sin, asks forgiveness, and extends forgiveness, pride loses oxygen. Corporate prayer also knits hearts together, because believers hear one another's needs and learn compassion again.

8) Protect Unity through Shared Worship and Shared Service

Unity grows when believers share a life, not only a meeting.

Shared worship centers hearts on God rather than on the self. Shared service reduces rivalry because you begin to see each other as fellow workers, not obstacles. When believers serve together, resentments often shrink because mission becomes larger than personality.

9) Strengthen Unity through Wise Leadership and Clear Commitment

Unity needs structure. The Spirit uses ordered leadership and clear commitments to protect the church.

Leaders must model humility and courage. They must correct false teaching, confront persistent sin, and refuse favoritism. They must also listen and treat members as people, not as problems.

Members must commit to the church's life. When people drift without real belonging, conflicts linger because there is no shared commitment to repair.

10) End with a Practical Rule: "Speak for Peace, Act for Peace"

If you want one rule that protects unity, use this: speak for peace and act for peace.

Speak for peace means your words aim at building, not scoring. It means you refuse gossip. It means you ask questions before you assume motives.

Act for peace means you take the first step when offense arises. It means you forgive quickly when repentance is real. It means you keep serving even when your feelings are mixed.

Unity is not a mood. It is a Spirit-produced life that believers protect through humility, truth, and patient love. When a church guards unity this way, it becomes a stable home for discipleship and a clear witness to Christ's reign.

BOOK FIVE

THE FUTURE: LIVE READY FOR CHRIST'S RETURN

A Simple Guide to Hope, Judgment, Resurrection, and the New Creation

CHAPTER 1

FIX YOUR HOPE ON CHRIST'S RETURN: LIVE WATCHFUL, FAITHFUL, AND UNAFRAID

Many people avoid end-times teaching because they have seen it misused. Some have heard predictions that failed. Others have watched believers argue about timelines with more heat than humility. Scripture calls you to a better approach: learn what God has clearly revealed, refuse speculation, and let hope shape how you live today.

The Christian future is not built on guesses. It is built on Christ's promise. The center is not a chart. The center is a Person who will return. When Scripture speaks about the end, it presses two truths at once: Christ's return is certain, and the timing is not for us to control. That combination is meant to produce readiness without panic.

1) Start with the Main Promise: Jesus Will Return

The New Testament treats Christ's return as normal Christian expectation. The church is not waiting for an idea. The church is waiting for its King.

Acts 1:11 (NSV) records the angels' words after Jesus ascended: this Jesus, who was taken up from you into heaven, will come in the same way as you saw Him go. The promise is direct. Jesus' return will be real, personal, and public.

That promise matters because it anchors hope in history. Christians are not trusting their ability to improve the world. Christians are trusting that Christ will finish what He began.

2) Know What "Return" Means: Christ Comes as Judge and Savior

Some people hear "judgment" and only think of terror. Scripture presents judgment as both sobering and good. It is good because evil will not rule forever. It is sobering because every person will answer to God.

2 Timothy 4:1 (NSV) says Christ Jesus will judge the living and the dead, and Paul charges Timothy to preach the word in light of that coming reality. Judgment is not a side doctrine. It shapes faithful ministry and holy living.

Yet the return is also salvation for God's people. Christ returns to complete rescue, not to restart it. Believers are not waiting to see if God will accept them. Believers are waiting to see the fullness of what God has promised.

3) Refuse Date-Setting: Read the Bible's Warnings About Speculation

Scripture tells you to be ready, not to be a predictor.

Matthew 24:36 (NSV) teaches that concerning that day and hour no one knows, not even angels in heaven, nor the Son, but the Father only. The point is not to make you indifferent. The point is to end the pride of secret knowledge.

Across church history, believers have repeatedly tried to fix dates, and those attempts have repeatedly failed. Wise teachers learned to emphasize what Scripture emphasizes: certainty of return, uncertainty of timing, and responsibility in the present.

4) Practice Readiness: Watchfulness Is a Lifestyle

If you cannot know the time, what should you do? Jesus answers: be ready.

1 Thessalonians 5:6 (NSV) calls believers to not sleep as others do, but to keep awake and be sober. The language is moral and spiritual, not literal insomnia. Watchfulness means you do not drift. You do not treat sin as harmless. You do not treat prayer as optional. You stay alert because you belong to Christ.

Watchfulness is also calm. A sober person is steady, not frantic. Christians should not live in constant alarm. They should live in daily faithfulness.

5) Hold a Clear Expectation: The Return Will Be Public and Final

Scripture does not describe Christ's return as a hidden event that only a few notice. It describes a decisive arrival that ends this present age.

Revelation 1:7 (NSV) says He is coming with the clouds, and every eye will see Him. The verse also reminds you that the return will confront rebellion. Christ's coming is comfort for believers and exposure for those who reject Him.

This public finality protects you from unhealthy fascination with rumors. The Bible directs you away from endless speculation and toward a simple readiness rooted in the gospel.

6) Learn How Christians Have Differed: Three Major Approaches

Faithful believers agree on the core: Christ will return, the dead will be raised, judgment will come, and God will make a new creation. Believers have differed on how to understand the timing of certain events, especially the "millennium" of Revelation 20. Here are three common views, stated fairly.

Amillennial view: Many believe the "millennium" describes Christ's present reign from heaven, with the church living between His first coming and His return. In this view, the focus is not on a future earthly thousand-year reign, but on Christ reigning now and returning once to judge and renew all things.

Postmillennial view: Some believe the gospel will advance broadly in history so that a long era of widespread Christian influence and peace occurs before Christ's return. In this view, Christ returns after that gospel-shaped era.

Premillennial view: Many believe Christ will return before a future millennium, understood as a distinct reign on earth. Within premillennial thought there are differences about how to read tribulation and the relationship between Israel and the church.

You do not need to choose a view quickly to live faithfully. Begin with what Scripture makes plain: Christ will return, and your task is readiness, not rivalry.

7) Let the Return Shape Holiness: Hope Produces Purity

A major purpose of end-times teaching is moral formation. Scripture links future hope with present purity.

1 John 3:2–3 (NSV) says that when Christ appears we shall be like Him, and everyone who hopes in Him purifies himself as He is pure. That is simple and strong. Hope is not passive. Hope trains the believer to resist sin because the believer belongs to a coming kingdom.

This also corrects a common excuse: "Since the end is coming, nothing matters." Scripture says the opposite. Since Christ is coming, everything matters. Your choices are training for eternity.

8) Let the Return Strengthen Endurance and Courage

Believers suffer in the present age, and Scripture does not hide it. The return of Christ means suffering is not the final chapter.

James 5:7–8 (NSV) tells believers to be patient until the coming of the Lord, establishing their hearts because the Lord's coming is near. "Near" here means certain and approaching, not a calendar prediction. The command is to establish your heart: plant your courage in God's promise.

This helps in ordinary trials. When life is unfair, you can endure without bitterness. When obedience costs you, you can persist without regret. Christ's return means faithfulness is never wasted.

9) Keep Your Focus: Readiness Is Ordinary Faithfulness

End-times readiness is not mainly about collecting information. It is about living clean, serving others, and staying close to Christ.

Readiness looks like this:

- Repent quickly when you sin.
- Forgive when you are wronged.
- Speak truth without cruelty.
- Work honestly.
- Pray steadily.
- Serve in the church.
- Share the gospel without shame.

This is how the early church lived. They confessed, "He will come again," and then they preached, endured persecution, cared for the needy, and worshiped with seriousness and joy.

10) End with the Future's Bright Center: God Will Make All Things New

The Bible's future is not endless clouds and vague spiritual existence. It is renewal.

Revelation 21:5 (NSV) records God's declaration: "Behold, I am making all things new." That promise does not minimize grief. It answers it. God does not discard His creation. He redeems it. The final hope is not escape from physical reality. It is the healing of reality under God's reign.

As we continue in Book 5, we will look closely at resurrection, judgment, and the new creation. For now, hold this as your daily anchor: Christ will return, and His return makes watchfulness wise, holiness necessary, and hope steady.

TRACE THE SPIRIT'S WORK IN THE OLD TESTAMENT: SEE GOD'S PRESENCE BEFORE PENTECOST

Many Christians assume the Holy Spirit appears only in the New Testament. Scripture does not support that idea. The Spirit is active from the opening lines of Genesis, and His work runs through Israel's history in ways that prepare you to understand Pentecost, the church, and the Christian life.

At the same time, the Old Testament and New Testament describe the Spirit's work with different emphases. In the Old Testament, the Spirit is often shown empowering particular people for particular tasks at particular times—kingship, craftsmanship, prophecy, leadership, and deliverance. In the New Testament, following Christ's finished work, the Spirit is poured out broadly on God's people in a fuller covenant sense. If you miss the Old Testament foundation, you may either downplay the Spirit's work or speak about it without biblical structure.

This chapter will trace the Spirit's work in the Old Testament under four headings: **creation, covenant life, empowerment for service, and promise of future outpouring**. Along the way, we will note how careful Christian teaching has drawn these themes together.

1) See the Spirit at Creation: God Brings Order and Life

The first time you meet the Spirit in Scripture is not in Acts. It is in Genesis.

Genesis 1:2 (NSV) describes the Spirit of God present over the waters as God prepares to bring order, beauty, and life. This verse teaches a basic truth: the Spirit is not a late addition to God's work. He is present at the beginning, active in creation.

The Bible reinforces this later. Job 33:4 (NSV) states, "The Spirit of God has made me, and the breath of the Almighty gives me life." Scripture connects the Spirit with life-giving power. He is not a distant concept. He is the divine giver of life and order.

This matters for theology and for daily faith. If the Spirit gives life in creation, then the Spirit giving life in salvation is consistent with who He is. New birth is not strange. It is God acting according to His nature.

2) Understand "Spirit" Language: Breath, Wind, and Presence

Old Testament language often uses words that carry the sense of breath or wind. The point is not poetic fog. The point is power and presence that cannot be controlled by human hands.

Wind is real, strong, and unseen. Breath is invisible yet essential for life. These images teach reverence. The Spirit is not a tool you can manage. He is God present and active.

This also protects you from treating spiritual life as technique. If the Spirit is God's living presence, then the right posture is dependence, prayer, obedience, and humility.

3) Trace the Spirit in Israel's Covenant Life: Guidance and Instruction

The Spirit is not only about extraordinary moments. The Old Testament shows the Spirit sustaining God's people through guidance and instruction.

Nehemiah 9:20 (NSV) praises God's mercy: God gave His good Spirit to instruct His people. That is striking. The Spirit is connected with teaching and formation, not only dramatic deliverances. God shepherds His people by His Spirit.

This also explains why Scripture and Spirit belong together. God's Spirit instructs in truth. He does not lead God's people into moral confusion. He forms them through God's Word, God's commands, and God's covenant purposes.

One of the most visible Old Testament themes is the Spirit empowering leaders for rescue and righteous action.

In the time of the judges, Scripture repeatedly states that the Spirit came upon a deliverer to rescue Israel from oppression. Judges 3:10 (NSV) says the Spirit of the Lord came upon Othniel, and he judged Israel and went out to war, and the Lord gave victory. The pattern repeats in the book: God raises a deliverer, empowers him, and rescues His people.

Two points matter here:

1. **The Spirit empowers for service, not self-display.** The goal is deliverance and protection of God's people, not personal fame.

2. **The Spirit's empowerment does not equal moral maturity.** Some judges were courageous yet deeply flawed. This warns you against equating visible gifting with holiness. God can empower a task without endorsing a person's character.

This is a practical lesson for today. A gifted leader may still require accountability. Spiritual power does not excuse sin. The Old Testament already teaches you to separate gifting from godliness.

5) See the Spirit Equip Craftsmanship: Skill for God's House

Many people think the Spirit only empowers "spiritual" activities like preaching. The Old Testament widens your view.

Exodus 31:2–5 (NSV) describes Bezalel being filled with the Spirit of God with ability, intelligence, knowledge, and craftsmanship to build for the tabernacle. That is Spirit-given skill in design, artistry, and construction for holy worship.

This expands your theology of vocation. The Spirit's work includes wisdom and skill used for God's glory. In modern terms, God can strengthen faithful work in teaching, administration, music, care, building, and problem-solving—especially when that work serves worship and the good of God's people.

This does not mean every talent is automatically spiritual. It means God is free to supply real ability for His purposes, and believers should honor skilled work as meaningful service.

6) Trace the Spirit in Kingship: Anointing, Rule, and Responsibility

The Spirit's relationship to kingship in the Old Testament is central for understanding Jesus as the anointed Messiah.

1 Samuel 16:13 (NSV) describes Samuel anointing David, and the Spirit of the Lord rushing upon him from that day forward. The Spirit's empowerment for David connects to leadership under God's authority. Israel's king was meant to rule in obedience to God, guarding justice and honoring the covenant.

Yet the Old Testament also warns that the Spirit's empowering presence in leadership could be forfeited in a covenantal sense through hardened rebellion. This is why David prays in Psalm 51:11 (NSV), "Do not cast me away from Your presence, and do not take Your Holy Spirit from me." David is not describing ordinary Christian experience after Pentecost in the same way. He is pleading as a covenant king who knows his sin threatens the stability of his calling and the wellbeing of the people he leads.

This is a key interpretive lesson: **Old Testament Spirit language often relates to roles—king, prophet, leader—within the covenant administration.** That prepares you to see why the New Testament later stresses the Spirit's indwelling of all believers as a shared covenant blessing.

7) See the Spirit in Prophecy: God Speaks Through His Servants

The prophets did not speak as private thinkers offering religious opinions. They spoke as God's messengers.

2 Peter 1:21 (NSV) states a New Testament summary of the Old Testament prophetic pattern: men spoke from God as they were carried along by the Holy Spirit. The Spirit is tied to revelation. God's Word comes by God's Spirit.

This is why the church has always treated Scripture as Spirit-given. It also explains why prophecy in Scripture is not merely encouragement. It includes rebuke, warning, and covenant instruction. The Spirit's work is not only comfort; it is truth.

The Old Testament shows God's real presence and real power, yet it also builds anticipation. Several passages look forward to a day when the Spirit's work would be more widespread and more inward.

Zechariah 4:6 (NSV) gives a famous principle: "Not by might, nor by power, but by My Spirit, says the Lord." This line addresses human weakness and God's sufficiency. It also points forward. God's work will not be secured by human strength. It will be secured by divine action.

The prophets also speak about a future era marked by deeper internal renewal. The Old Testament repeatedly connects hope with a change of heart and a greater work of God among His people. This prepares you for the New Testament's language about new birth, indwelling, and Spirit-given transformation across the whole church.

9) Learn from Israel's Failure: The Spirit Can Be Resisted and Grieved

The Old Testament is candid about rebellion. God's people often received mercy and still resisted God.

Isaiah 63:10 (NSV) says they rebelled and grieved His Holy Spirit. That verse is important because it holds two truths together: the Spirit is personal, and resistance is real. People can oppose God's leading. They can harden their hearts. They can reject instruction.

This prepares you to understand why the New Testament includes both comfort and warning. The Spirit strengthens believers, and believers are also commanded not to resist, quench, or ignore His work. The covenant story teaches that spiritual privilege never justifies spiritual carelessness.

10) Connect Old Testament Themes to Christ: The Spirit Prepares the Way

The Old Testament's Spirit-work is not isolated. It is preparation for Christ.

- The Spirit gives life in creation, preparing you to see the Spirit give life in regeneration.
- The Spirit empowers leaders and kings, preparing you for the Messiah, the true anointed King.

- The Spirit speaks through prophets, preparing you for Christ, the final Word and faithful Prophet.
- The Spirit instructs and guides the people, preparing you for a fuller covenant community shaped from within.

In church history, this is one reason theologians spoke about the unity of God's saving work: the Spirit's presence is consistent, yet His covenant administration unfolds with the storyline. The Old Testament is not "Spirit-less." It is "promise-shaped." It creates categories that become clearer after Christ's death, resurrection, and ascension.

11) Apply This Chapter: Live with Reverence, Gratitude, and Wise Expectations

Here are three practical ways this Old Testament view helps you today.

First, it keeps you from treating the Spirit as novelty.

The Spirit has been active from the beginning. You do not need constant new claims to take Him seriously.

Second, it teaches you to value character above gifting.

Judges and kings show that empowerment for a task does not guarantee holiness. Do not confuse visible ability with spiritual maturity.

Third, it teaches you to seek the Spirit's help in ordinary work.

The Spirit equipped Bezalel for craftsmanship. Pray for wisdom, skill, patience, and faithfulness in the work God has given you.

The Old Testament teaches that God's Spirit is real, personal, and powerful: present in creation, guiding covenant life, empowering service, and promising deeper renewal.

CHAPTER 3

FOLLOW THE SPIRIT IN JESUS' LIFE: SEE THE MESSIAH ANOINTED FOR HIS MISSION

If you want to understand the Holy Spirit, do not begin with debates or unusual claims. Begin with Jesus. The Spirit's work in Christ's life shows what true anointing looks like: it produces holiness, truth, compassion, and faithful obedience to the Father. It also shows that salvation is not only about what Jesus did *for* you on the cross, but also about what He did *as* the obedient Messiah—living, resisting temptation, proclaiming the kingdom, and carrying out His mission by the Spirit's power.

This chapter will trace the Spirit's role in Jesus' life from conception to ministry to sacrifice. The goal is to help you see the Spirit's work with biblical clarity and to apply it wisely to Christian life today.

1) Start at the Beginning: The Spirit's Work in the Incarnation

Jesus did not begin His existence in Bethlehem. He is the eternal Son who took on human nature. Yet the incarnation enters history through the Spirit's work.

Luke 1:35 (NSV) explains to Mary that the Holy Spirit will come upon her, and the power of the Most High will overshadow her. This is not an abstract miracle. It is God preparing a true human nature for the Son, in a holy and unique way. The Spirit's work here guards two truths: Jesus is truly human, and He is holy from the start.

This matters for salvation because a Savior who shares our humanity can represent us, and a Savior who is sinless can save us.

2) Notice the Pattern: The Spirit Marks Jesus as the Promised Messiah

In the Old Testament, kings were anointed as a sign of divine appointment. Jesus is "the Christ," the Anointed One, and the Spirit's presence marks His identity and mission.

At Jesus' baptism, the Spirit descends on Him. Luke 3:21–22 (NSV) describes the Spirit coming in bodily form like a dove, and the Father's voice declaring Jesus as His beloved Son. This event is Trinitarian, public, and decisive. It shows that Jesus' mission begins with divine confirmation.

The Spirit's descent does not mean Jesus lacked deity before baptism. Jesus is eternally the Son. Rather, it shows Jesus beginning His public ministry as the Messiah, equipped for His role as the obedient servant-king.

3) See the Spirit Lead Jesus into Testing: Holiness Before Public Power

Many people chase public power while neglecting holiness. Jesus' path is the reverse. The Spirit leads Him into testing before public ministry.

Luke 4:1–2 (NSV) says Jesus, full of the Holy Spirit, was led by the Spirit in the wilderness. This is important. Temptation is not always a sign God is absent. Sometimes it is part of God's shaping work. Jesus faces real temptation, not as a sinner, but as the righteous Messiah who must succeed where Adam and Israel failed.

He resists by Scripture. He does not argue with clever philosophy. He stands on God's Word. This teaches you that the Spirit's leading will not separate you from Scripture. The Spirit strengthens obedience, and Scripture provides the clear line.

4) Hear Jesus Describe His Ministry: The Spirit Anoints for Good News and Mercy

Jesus does not leave you guessing about the Spirit's role in His mission. He explains it openly.

Luke 4:18–19 (NSV) records Jesus reading from Isaiah: the Spirit of the Lord is upon Me because He has anointed Me to preach good news to the poor, proclaim liberty to captives, recovery of sight to the blind, and freedom to the oppressed. Then Jesus says this Scripture is fulfilled in their hearing.

This is one of the most important Spirit passages in the Gospels. It shows the Spirit's anointing leads to:

- proclamation of good news,
- mercy to the weak,

- liberation from bondage,
- visible signs that confirm the kingdom's arrival.

The focus is not spectacle. The focus is the kingdom of God advancing through truth and compassion.

5) Understand Miracles as Signs of the Kingdom, Not Performances

Jesus' miracles are not random displays of ability. They are signs that God's reign has arrived and that the curse is being reversed.

When Jesus heals, restores, and delivers, He is showing what God's kingdom does. In doing so, He also shows that spiritual power is meant for service. Jesus' miracles do not create ego. They create worship, gratitude, and amazement at God's mercy.

This corrects a modern temptation: to treat spiritual power as status. In Christ, power serves love. Any claim of Spirit-power that produces pride, manipulation, or harm is already out of step with Jesus.

6) See the Spirit and the Father's Will Working Together

In Jesus' life, the Spirit's power never competes with the Father's will. The Spirit leads Jesus into obedience, suffering, and faithful endurance.

Jesus' ministry includes joy and compassion, but it also includes conflict, rejection, and ultimately the cross. The Spirit's presence does not guarantee an easy path. It guarantees faithful obedience and divine strength to complete the mission.

This matters for believers. If you assume the Spirit's presence means life will be simple, you will become confused when hardship comes. Jesus' Spirit-filled life included suffering with purpose.

7) Understand Christ's Obedience as Representative: He Succeeds Where We Failed

Jesus lived in full obedience not only as an example, but also as the representative Messiah. He stands in the place of His people. His obedience fulfills righteousness.

This connects the Spirit's work to salvation directly. The Spirit empowered Jesus' human life for obedient service. Then Jesus offers His obedient life and atoning death as the ground of salvation.

This is not a small detail. If Jesus is only an example, you are left trying to imitate Him without hope. If Jesus is Savior and representative, you can imitate Him from a secure position, not to earn acceptance.

8) Learn What True Anointing Produces: Fruit Before Gifts

If you want a simple test of Spirit-work, look at Jesus:

- humility instead of self-promotion,
- truth instead of manipulation,
- compassion instead of contempt,
- purity instead of compromise,
- endurance instead of quitting.

This does not mean gifts are unimportant. It means fruit is the first evidence of the Spirit's work. Gifts can be counterfeited or misused. Christlike character cannot be faked for long.

A church that seeks gifts without seeking Christlike character will eventually drift into confusion. A believer who seeks experiences without seeking holiness will eventually be disappointed.

9) Connect Jesus' Ministry to the Promise of the Spirit for Believers

Jesus' Spirit-anointed life is not meant to remain unique and distant. It prepares for the Spirit's outpouring on the church.

Jesus promises that His followers will receive the Spirit in a new covenant fullness after His work is finished. The Gospels present Jesus as the one who baptizes with the Holy Spirit, bringing God's presence to His people in a deeper way.

So the Spirit's work in Jesus is both model and foundation: it shows what Spirit-empowered faithfulness looks like, and it prepares the way for believers to live by the Spirit as those united to Christ.

10) Apply This Chapter: Follow Christ's Pattern in Three Ways

First, pursue holiness before influence.

The Spirit led Jesus into the wilderness before the crowds. Do not rush past hidden obedience.

Second, tie guidance to Scripture.

Jesus resisted temptation with God's Word. Do not treat impressions as higher than Scripture.

Third, serve with compassion.

Jesus' Spirit-anointed ministry brought good news to the poor and help to the afflicted. Measure your "spiritual life" by whether it produces patient love.

When you study the Spirit in Jesus' life, you gain a stable picture of true Spirit-work. It is not chaotic. It is not self-centered. It is Christ-centered and Father-pleasing. In the next chapter, we will move from Jesus' ministry to the Spirit's arrival in the early church, especially at Pentecost, and we will see what changed and what remained consistent with the Old Testament foundation.

CHAPTER 4

STUDY VIEWS WITH CHARITY: COMPARE MAJOR END - TIMES FRAMEWORKS FAIRLY

Christians who love Scripture have not always agreed on how to arrange end-times details. That fact should not surprise you. Some passages are direct and simple. Others are symbolic and require careful reading. The church's best teachers have urged believers to hold tight to what is clear, and to handle debated points with humility.

Here is the baseline every faithful framework must keep:

- Jesus will return bodily and publicly.
- The dead will be raised.
- Final judgment will come.
- God will renew creation and dwell with His people.
- The gospel must be preached to the nations, and believers must endure.

Within that shared center, Christians differ mainly on how they interpret **Revelation 20** (the "thousand years"), the relationship between Christ's return and that millennium, and how to understand tribulation language.

1) Begin with the "Clear Core" Before the "Complex Map"

When believers argue, it is often because they start with disputed details instead of shared truths. Scripture gives you a better order. Start with what the whole Bible repeats often, then work outward.

A helpful anchor is **2 Peter 3:10–13 (NSV)**, which describes the day of the Lord, God's judgment, and the promise of "new heavens and a new earth." Whatever your end-times view, it must fit that movement: Christ returns, evil is judged, and creation is renewed.

Revelation 20:1–6 (NSV) is the key text that drives the big differences. Christians ask: Is this "thousand years" a present reality, a future era, or a symbolic description of a long period?

A. Amillennial view

- "Millennium" is understood as the present reign of Christ from heaven during the church age.

- Satan is restrained in a real sense, so the gospel can go to the nations.

- Christ returns once, bringing resurrection and judgment, followed by the new creation.

Why many find it persuasive: it ties Revelation 20 tightly to the New Testament theme of Christ reigning now and returning in a single climactic event.

B. Postmillennial view

- The "millennium" is often understood as a long era (not necessarily exactly 1,000 years) in which the gospel's influence expands widely.

- Christ returns after that era, followed by final judgment and renewal.

Why many find it persuasive: it emphasizes the power of the gospel to spread and shape nations over time, and it reads certain kingdom promises with strong historical optimism.

C. Premillennial view

- Christ returns before a future millennium, understood as a distinct reign.

- After the millennium comes a final judgment and then the new creation.

Why many find it persuasive: it reads Revelation 20's sequence more straightforwardly and often links it to Old Testament kingdom promises.

3) Recognize Two Major Premillennial Families

Premillennialism is not one uniform view.

Historic premillennialism often emphasizes continuity between Israel and the church and reads tribulation as a reality the church may face.

Dispensational premillennialism more sharply distinguishes Israel and the church and often includes a framework for tribulation and end-times events that differs from historic premillennialism.

Faithful believers exist in both groups. The practical takeaway is to listen carefully before assuming what someone means by "premillennial."

4) Handle the Tribulation with Care

Scripture speaks plainly about suffering and pressure for believers. The question is how to place certain "tribulation" texts in a timeline.

A responsible approach does three things:

- It refuses panic.
- It prepares believers for endurance and faithfulness.
- It resists turning every headline into a prophecy key.

John 16:33 (NSV) keeps a steady tone: in the world you will have tribulation, but take heart; Christ has overcome the world. That is not a timeline. It is an endurance promise.

5) Avoid Two Common Mistakes

Mistake 1: Treating a framework as the gospel.

Your framework must serve Scripture, not replace it. The gospel is Christ crucified and risen, calling sinners to repent and believe.

Mistake 2: Treating disagreements as disloyalty to Christ.

Many differences are real, but they are not always worth breaking fellowship. A church should have clarity, but believers should also show restraint and honor.

6) Practice Charity Without Becoming Vague

Charity does not mean "anything goes." It means you speak fairly, you summarize opposing views accurately, and you do not assign motives. You can say, "I disagree," without saying, "You reject Scripture."

If you want a simple rule:

be firm about Christ's return and careful about disputed sequences.

CHAPTER 5

LONG FOR THE NEW CREATION: SEE HEAVEN AND EARTH MADE NEW

Many people picture the Christian future as floating souls, endless clouds, and a vague spiritual calm. Scripture offers something better: **new creation**. God will renew heaven and earth, remove the curse, and dwell with His people in open fellowship.

The Bible's final hope is not escape from physical reality. It is the healing of reality under Christ's reign.

1) Start with God's Promise: Renewal, Not Disposal

Isaiah spoke of a future where God creates "new heavens and a new earth." **Isaiah 65:17 (NSV)** presents that promise in direct terms. The language is not about God abandoning His world. It is about God restoring it.

This changes how you live now. What God plans to renew, you must not despise. Creation matters. Bodies matter. Work matters. Justice matters. These things are not ultimate, but they are meaningful.

2) Understand "Heaven" as God's Dwelling, Then God's Dwelling With Us

Scripture often uses "heaven" to refer to God's realm and presence. The Bible's end is not believers going up forever while earth is discarded. The end is God's dwelling with His people in renewed creation.

Revelation 21:1–4 (NSV) describes a new heaven and new earth, the holy city coming down, and God dwelling with His people. It also states that God will wipe away every tear, and death will be no more. The future is personal: comfort, healing, and removal of the curse.

3) Take Comfort in What Will Be Removed

New creation is not only about what you gain. It is about what God removes:

- death
- mourning
- crying
- pain
- corruption
- injustice

That removal matters because many believers carry grief that does not resolve in this life. Scripture does not insult that grief. It answers it with promise.

4) See Holiness as Home, Not Burden

Some people fear eternity because they imagine it as endless rules. Scripture presents it as holy joy. In the new creation, holiness will not feel like strain, because sin will no longer pull the heart in competing directions.

Revelation 22:3–5 (NSV) describes the removal of the curse, worship, and God's people reigning forever. That is not boredom. It is life finally ordered as it should be: worship, purpose, and peace.

5) Let New Creation Reshape Suffering

If the end is renewal, then suffering is not meaningless. It is real, and it hurts, but it is not the final word.

Romans 8:18–23 (NSV) describes creation's groaning and the believer's longing for redemption. Scripture gives language for waiting without pretending. The future does not erase present pain, but it does keep pain from becoming your master.

6) Live with "Future-Faithfulness"

The hope of new creation does not make Christians passive. It makes them steady. You can endure hardship without despair, because you are headed toward restoration. You can serve without needing applause, because your labor is not wasted. You can forgive, because justice will be done.

New creation hope forms a people who are difficult to corrupt, because they are not desperate to squeeze heaven out of the present age.

CHAPTER 6

LIVE READY NOW: PRACTICE FAITHFULNESS, WATCHFULNESS, AND JOY

The New Testament does not teach readiness as fear-driven survival. It teaches readiness as steady faithfulness. You live ready by staying close to Christ, turning from sin quickly, serving your neighbors, and doing your daily work with integrity.

Readiness is not mainly about knowing more information. It is about living with the return of Christ in view.

1) Choose Watchfulness Over Speculation

Jesus calls His people to be ready, not to predict.

Luke 12:35–37 (NSV) pictures servants dressed for action, lamps burning, awaiting their master. The emphasis is simple: live in a state of spiritual readiness. Do not drift into carelessness.

Watchfulness means:

- you keep repentance close,
- you keep prayer regular,
- you keep conscience tender,
- you keep Christ's commands in view.

2) Practice Faithfulness in Ordinary Work

Many believers think readiness means doing "religious" tasks only. Scripture teaches readiness in daily labor and daily responsibilities.

Colossians 3:23–24 (NSV) calls believers to work heartily, as for the Lord and not for men, knowing they will receive an inheritance from the Lord. That passage turns ordinary work into worship. Faithfulness is not glamorous, but it is deeply Christian.

3) Hold Joy as a Duty and a Gift

Christian joy is not denial. It is confidence in Christ's reign and promise. Joy grows when you stop demanding that this present age provide what only the new creation will provide.

Titus 2:11–13 (NSV) ties daily life to future hope: grace trains believers to live self-controlled, upright, and godly lives while waiting for the blessed hope—the appearing of Jesus Christ. Notice the structure: grace trains, and hope steadies.

4) Refuse the Two Readiness Traps

Trap 1: Alarm.

Alarm reads every event as a secret sign and produces anxiety. Scripture calls for sobriety, not panic.

Trap 2: Sleep.

Sleep treats sin lightly, prayer lightly, and church life lightly. Scripture calls for alertness.

Readiness is neither frantic nor careless. It is steady.

5) Invest in What Will Last

A ready life puts energy into what endures:

- truth
- love
- holiness
- mercy
- gospel witness
- church faithfulness
- generosity

1 Corinthians 15:58 (NSV) calls believers to be steadfast and always abounding in the work of the Lord, knowing their labor is not in vain. That verse is grounded in resurrection hope. It is not motivational talk. It is a future-based promise.

If you want a practical readiness plan, use this daily rule:

- **Confess**: ask God to expose sin quickly.
- **Trust**: rehearse one clear gospel truth about Christ.
- **Obey**: do one specific act of obedience before the day ends.
- **Serve**: do one act of love that costs time or pride.
- **Hope**: end the day remembering Christ will return.

OVERALL CONCLUSION
HOLD TO CHRIST, LIVE WITH CLARITY, AND FINISH WELL

Systematic theology is not a shelf item for scholars. It is a steady guide for ordinary believers who want to know God, love Him, and follow Him with confidence. Over these five Books, you have traced the central truths of the Christian faith: God's character and works, humanity's dignity and fall, salvation in Christ, the Holy Spirit's presence and ministry, and the future God has promised.

These doctrines belong together. When you separate them, faith becomes unstable. When you hold them together, faith becomes grounded. You learn to worship God as He truly is, not as culture imagines Him to be. You learn to see yourself honestly—created in God's image, yet in need of grace. You learn to trust Christ as the only Savior whose life, death, and resurrection secure real forgiveness and real peace with God. You learn to reflect on the Holy Spirit not as a vague influence, but as God who applies salvation, strengthens holiness, equips the church, and comforts believers in suffering. And you learn to look to the future without fear, because Christ will return, judgment will be just, resurrection will be real, and God will renew all things.

The aim of this book has never been information alone. The aim is transformation that rests on truth. Sound doctrine produces humble worship, clear repentance, steady obedience, and resilient hope. It trains you to live in the present age without being ruled by it. It helps you love the church with patience, serve others with integrity, and face hardship without surrendering to despair. Above all, it keeps your eyes on Christ— the center of Scripture, the head of the church, and the Lord of history.

As you close this volume, do not treat it as finished work that belongs behind you. Treat it as a framework you return to. Revisit the chapters. Open your Bible. Pray with purpose. Practice what you have learned. The Christian life is not sustained by intensity, but by daily faithfulness. God is faithful, and He will keep His people.

May the Lord strengthen you to think clearly, love deeply, and live ready—until the day you see Christ face to face.